Columbia University

Contributions to Education

Teachers College Series

No. 436

2 16 710

AMS PRESS
NEW YORK

THE EFFECTIVENESS OF MODERN SPELLING INSTRUCTION

BY

ROBERT S. THOMPSON, Ph.D.

TEACHERS COLLEGE, COLUMBIA UNIVERSITY
CONTRIBUTIONS TO EDUCATION, No. 436

BUREAU OF PUBLICATIONS
Teachers College, Columbia University
NEW YORK CITY
1930

Library of Congress Cataloging in Publication Data

Thompson, Robert Sydney, 1892–
    The effectiveness of modern spelling instruction.

    Reprint of the 1930 ed., issued in series: Teachers
College, Columbia University. Contributions to
education, no. 436.
    Originally presented as the author's thesis, Columbia.
    Bibliography: p.
    1. English language—Orthography and spelling.
I. Title. II. Series: Columbia University. Teachers
College. Contributions to education, no. 436.
LB1574.T4 1972   372.6'32   72-177717
ISBN 0-404-55436-9

Reprinted by Special Arrangement with Teachers
College Press, New York, New York

From the edition of 1930, New York
First AMS edition published in 1972
Manufactured in the United States

AMS PRESS, INC.
NEW YORK, N. Y.   10003

ACKNOWLEDGMENTS

It is with some diffidence that the author records here his obligations to the chairman of his dissertation committee, Professor Arthur I. Gates. Such an acknowledgment might plausibly be suspected as an attempt to support the obvious shortcomings of the study with the prestige of Professor Gates' name. However, I owe so much to Professor Gates, quite apart from this study, that it may be proper to express my appreciation for the stimulus to personal and professional growth that his patient counseling and high example have afforded me.

To Professor Edwin H. Reeder I am grateful for kindly advice and encouragement; to Professor Ralph Spence for valuable criticism.

Principal Frederick B. Graham and Assistant Principal Leonard of Public School No. 210, Brooklyn, New York, have generously made available all the facilities of the school for the experimental work and have given liberally of their time and professional wisdom.

My wife, Lois M. Thompson, has devoted many hours to wearying and monotonous statistical computation and clerical work. But it has been her never failing encouragement that has made the completion of the study possible.

R. S. T.

CONTENTS

THE EFFECTIVENESS OF MODERN SPELLING INSTRUCTION

CHAPTER I

REVIEW OF EXPERIMENTAL INVESTIGATIONS

Even the most cursory survey of the educational articles dealing with English spelling during the last generation must convince the student that the subject is highly complex. Theorists who have been fortunate in a special aptitude, or who have forgotten their early struggles with the subject, have sometimes been disposed to consider the matter a simple one. In such quarters the psychology of spelling is dismissed as being compassed by the principle of attentive repetition, its measurement by the checking of the number of words wrong, and its methods by the liberal use of drill. This view is easily understandable as issuing from the fact that spelling is concerned only with single words and the writing of the letters of the words in order. With such simple and definite units and such a well-defined goal, is not the matter clear and simple?

On the other hand, seasoned investigators, impressed by the capricious performance of words and the impossibility of finding a logical system of organization to guide the learning, have promulgated the dogma that each word is a law unto itself, and its learning is a strictly specific matter. Hence the laborious search for the most frequently used words and the emphasis upon individual study of the words which the pupil misses. This dogma has been highly fruitful. There is, however, a rising suspicion that it has been emphasized to a fault.

The paramount need is a thoroughgoing scientific analysis of the psychology of spelling. Neither more nor better methods of drill, nor the most ingenious methods of individual and specific attack on words will make up for an ignorance of exactly how the learning of spelling goes on, incidentally and within the spelling period. A good beginning has been made by Hollingworth [25]* and Gates [19].

* Bracketed numbers throughout this study refer to items listed in the Bibliography.

1

In any effort at appraisal of the place, methods, and psychology of spelling, one is struck by the fact that scientific warrant for many of the most confidently followed practices is not infrequently lacking, or is equivocal. A recently published bibliography lists 296 titles and one investigator reports that she consulted more than three hundred items. Many of these references report upon experimental data, but the conclusions arrived at are often conflicting, or the data are inadequate to carry the burden of the solutions loaded on them. On the other hand, a not inconsiderable portion of the literature occupies itself with the airing of opinions highly controversial in character. Such titles as, "A Modern Babel," "A Pestiferous Subject," and "Our Accursed Spelling," furnish intimations of the temper of some of the discussions.

Illustrations of the conflicting counsels and implications of some of the outstanding investigations that have been carried on in the past will serve the double purpose of bringing to the reader's attention the need for exact analysis and of making clear the aims of the present investigation. No attempt will be made to present an exhaustive survey of the literature. That has been done in other places. Only those investigations which promise to be helpful in interpreting the writer's own data will be reviewed.

The revolutionary investigations of Rice [45] are too well known to need extended description. Their importance does not lie in the specific findings, but in the inauguration of the objective method and the courage displayed in attacking current educational idols. His conclusions have been subjected to close scrutiny. (See Tidyman [53].) His findings with respect to the relationship of spelling to age, heredity, home environment, method, and personality of the teacher have been shown to be insecure. With respect, however, to the conclusions as to the relationship between spelling efficiency and school time allotted to spelling, the most severe critical assault has not shaken his position. There are few efficient schools to-day that devote more than fifteen minutes a day to spelling—the maximum recommended by Rice. Furthermore, his raising of the question of economy of time inspired two decades of experimental work in which economy of time was the leading general objective.

Inspired by Rice's study, Cornman [16] undertook the experiment of dropping the spelling period and confining spelling instruction to incidental teaching. "Words liable to be misspelled were placed conspicuously before the pupils when they were engaged upon an exercise in which the words were likely to occur; pupils were taught to appeal, when in doubt, to the teachers and [those of higher grades] to the dictionary and mistakes in written work were corrected as far as possible."

This program was carried out for three years, beginning June, 1897, and ending June, 1900. Summing up the results of his investigation, he flatly states, "The conclusion, therefore, is forced upon us that an influence, the suspension of whose operation for three years is not plainly manifested in such a series of tests as those described above, is of so little importance as to be practically negligible."

It is unfortunate that Cornman's conclusions were either accepted somewhat uncritically as demonstrating the superiority of the method of incidental teaching, or were strenuously attacked on the ground of the techniques employed. The partisans of drill and of incidental teaching waged a verbal war during the first decade of the century until Wallin's findings [57] seemed to tip the balance for a time to the side of drill. A generation later it seems that the issues suggested were much more profound than merely the respective merits of two general methods of teaching.

One of these issues is the matter of incidental learning as distinguished from the mere method of incidental teaching. Cornman attributed his results to incidental *teaching*. A generation later we are more impressed with the importance of incidental learning in spelling and there is a growing suspicion that the secret of spelling success lies less in the specific instruction of the spelling period than in methods and learnings that accompany reading, writing, etc. The other issue involves fundamentals in the philosophy of measurement and a new definition of spelling. Before developing these questions, let us briefly recall Cornman's experiment.

During the three-year period of suspension of instruction in spelling, several types of tests were used to determine the achievements of the pupils. One of the types was the ordinary column test; another was a more interesting one which had been adapted from Rice. His "composition" test was a composition on an assigned topic such as "A Trip to Fairmount Park," or an essay written in answer to a question in geography, grammar, science, or history. The measure of spelling ability was the percentage of correctly spelled words in the composition, using as a base for the calculation the total number of words written. If the same word was misspelled several times, each misspelling was counted. The median length of the compositions varied from about 90 words in the third grade to about 400 words in the seventh grade. The table below summarizes the spelling situation at the beginning and at the end of the three-year period when evaluated by the composition tests.

TABLE 1

The Effect of the Suspension of the Regular Spelling Period as Disclosed by Composition Tests (After Cornman)

DATE	PRIMARY GRADES			UPPER GRADES		
	Median Number Pupils	Median Number Words	Median Percentage Correct	Median Number Pupils	Median Number Words	Median Percentage Correct
June, 1897	154	104	95.3	349	189	98.2
May, 1900	195	150	94.3	290	213	98.8

The table reads as follows: At the beginning of the period of suspension of direct teaching, June, 1897, 154 pupils in the primary grades wrote compositions of the median length of 104 words and spelled the total number of words in the composition with a median correctness of 95.3 per cent. From Table 1 it appears that spelling achievement, measured after this fashion, was unaffected by the suspension of formal instruction.

The other sort of test employed was the ordinary column test. The words, of course, were not of the pupil's own selection. These tests were characteristic of the period in that they contained many hard, unusual words. Some of these tests were given as term examinations in spelling in a number of other schools. Thus a comparison of results in the two experimental schools and in the other city schools was possible. The results summarized in Table 2 are representative.

The two experimental schools seem to have passed from a position of slight superiority to one of slight inferiority to the other city schools during the period of suspension of direct instruction. The statistical significance of these differences was not given. If the differences were real, would they be of much practical importance? In the first place, it should not be expected that children who had had no practice in list spelling for three years would do quite so well as those who had, other things being equal. In the second place, the children of the other schools had presumably studied the words of the examinations during the school year, while it was probably a matter of chance whether or not the children of the experimental schools had encountered the words. Had the tests been repeated after the summer vacation when all recency value of the specific instruction had been dissipated the results might have been different.

Cornman's experiment is a generation away. Conditions have changed too much in the interim to permit any direct comparison with what is achieved to-day. Principles of statistical and experimental research since developed do not support his technique. But after all such allowances are made, the underlying fact stands forth that in the upper grades between 98 and 99 per cent of the words written in spontaneous composition by the children were spelled correctly.

From the standpoint of scientific method, measurement by composition tests may in certain respects be lacking in scientific exactitude and the results may be hard to interpret comparatively; but the ability to spell in written composition is certainly the ultimate aim of the teaching of spelling. It is the aim not only in school composition, of course, but in all sorts of spontaneous com-

TABLE 2

A COMPARISON OF THE RESULTS OF THE INCIDENTAL METHOD WITH THOSE
OF THE CONVENTIONAL METHOD (AFTER CORNMAN)

GRADE	MEDIAN PERCENTAGE OF WORDS CORRECT			
	January, 1898		June, 1900	
	11 Schools	2 Experimental Schools	50 Schools	2 Experimental Schools
Grades 3–4	65.5	66.7	75.5	68.1
Grades 5–8	73.7	76.6	71.7	69.9
All grades	71.4	72.3	73.0	69.0

positions. If spelling ability is defined as the ability to write the letters of words in correct order upon dictation, and if the test of an individual's ability is his proficiency in spelling all the words in the dictionary, or all the words the teacher thinks he should know, or the three, five, or ten thousand most commonly used words, then composition tests are not proper instruments for such measurement. It is then easy to point out that in composition tests there may be a tendency for the child to restrict his writing to words he knows how to spell; that many easy words such as *the, and, is, it, you,* etc., are used over and over so that a composition of three or four hundred words may not contain very many different words; that only a few experiences can be dealt with in compositions and that the words are, therefore, limited to those useful in expressing those experiences. It might also be said that the spelling instruction then in vogue was ineffective and might well have been omitted without loss. Rice characterizes the methods in general use as follows:

The absurdities incident to the so-called "natural" method were shown very clearly during one of my visits to a fifth year class, in which the pupils, who had studied the pine, were about to write a composition on the subject. In preparation, the spelling lesson of the day consisted of the following words: exogen, erect, cylindrical, coniferal, irregular, indestructible, pins, resinous, and whorls.[1]

However, if spelling ability is defined as the ability to write the words one needs in composing his letters, reports, minutes, etc., which he composes in the course of his social and business affairs, the composition test has the virtue of being much the same thing. A child who acquired the habit of practically 100 per cent correct spelling in everything he wrote would not cause anxiety as to particular words he could not spell.

To put the matter in a different way, the composition test may be viewed from two angles. From the angle of statistical measurement it is defective because the results from different individuals are not comparable and because it gives no measure of "absolute" spelling ability—that is, the spelling of all words that some individuals of a certain social group might need to spell. Viewed from the other angle, that of child development and expression, the composition test is a valid measure of "functioning" spelling ability for it checks the child on the word his individual development demands for expression. If the matter is viewed in its larger

[1] *Scientific Management in Education*, p. 63.

implications, it involves two often conflicting approaches to education: the sociological, which emphasizes social processes and group standards, and the psychological, which stresses individual differences and individual students.

This sounds, perhaps, as if the substantial achievements in the field of standardized tests were to be dismissed because they subject individuals to mass standards and because it is impossible to set up group standards of educational progress. Far from it. We need the tests, but we also need to know the relationship of the abilities measured by the test to the ability that functions in the life situation. In spelling this means that it is necessary to know to what extent the child's ability to spell a dictated list of words immediately after study, or a month after study, or at the end of the school year in which the words are studied, is the same thing as correct spelling of the words of his social and business correspondence as an adult, or even of his school day letters, compositions, examinations, etc.

One aspect of the problem is the same as that which arose in connection with the interpretation of tests of general intelligence. In the first enthusiasm of the movement it was thought that the tests did really test "general intelligence" and that in so far as tasks were intellectual, the tests gave a reliable measure of one's ability in and out of school. It was rather naïvely assumed that the thing measured by the tests was the thing that was necessary to success in widely varied fields. It is now quite generally admitted that different intelligence tests measure somewhat different abilities and that the worth of a test lies in the correlation found between the abilities it measures and the abilities required for success in the field in which the test is being used to predict. Thus certain intelligence tests have been found to be highly reliable in predicting school success but not business success.

This phase of the matter might be thought of as a problem of transfer. The question would be one of the degree to which spelling learned in school functions outside of school. However, transfer in this sense should not be confused with the sort of transfer that has been commonly investigated in spelling. Wallin [58], for example, studied the question of the degree of transfer exhibited when words learned in column form were spelled by children in the writing of the same word in dictated compositions. Others have thought it necessary to dictate sentences to children in order to get a true measure of the ability to spell. It is not transfer in this narrow sense that is here referred to. It is transfer in the sense that school spelling of the spelling period translates itself into ability to spell what one may write out of school. The two abilities are not the same.

However, it might be more fruitful to think of the matter in terms of the permanence of learning. The problem would then be stated in this manner. To what extent, with respect to the words taught during the term, does the ability to spell them, immediately, a week, a month after study, or at the end of the school term, persist when the individual writes in life situations after leaving school, or even later in his school course? The question might be partly answered by studying the permanent effects of the teaching of spelling even when measured in the ordinary school fashion.

Data bearing on the issue of how well students spell in various types of written material have been gathered by some investigators. These data furnish some evidence of the permanent effects of the teaching of spelling.

Ashbaugh [5] examined 300 letters written by children to other children. The seventh, ninth, and twelfth grades were each represented by 100 letters. In the seventh grade the percentage of running words misspelled was 2.6; in the ninth, 1.7; in the twelfth, 1.4. These percentages approximate those found by Cornman for the fifth, sixth, seventh, and eighth grades in his composition tests after three years of no specific instruction. Of course, the results are not strictly comparable because children may be more on guard when writing test compositions than when writing letters to other children.

Brandenberg [9] found that a college class in mental development misspelled, on the average, 5.2 words per student in final examination papers averaging 1,667 words in length. This is only a percentage of .003 misspelled. However, it should be borne in mind that the class submitted eighteen written papers during the semester in this subject. Considerable practice in spelling certain words peculiar to the subject must have been had.

Hilderbrant [24] had the compositions of 15,500 students in sixteen high schools examined for misspelling. These compositions were written within a period of fifteen minutes on subjects of the student's own choosing. The high schools were described as among the best in the United States. The author does not give percentages of errors for the number of words written. The percentage of misspellings can be computed from her figures, however. On the average, each student misspelled 1.2 per cent of the words he wrote. These composition tests were evidently quite similar to Cornman's. It is quite significant that the spelling of these high school students in their compositions is no better than that of Cornman's fifth, sixth, seventh, and eighth grade pupils if the composition test is a good test. Presumably all these students had had years of specific spelling instruction.

Lester [36] studied the English examination papers of 2,414 students who took the College Entrance Board Examinations in the years 1913–1919. Misspellings of the same word were counted only once unless there was a variation of the misspelling. (Cornman counted all misspellings.) Lester's figures show that 2,602 different words were misspelled and there was a total of 14,505 misspellings of these words. As there were approximately 1,378,-000 running words written in the examination papers, the percentage of misspellings was about 1.0 per cent of the total number of running words. This percentage is practically the same as Cornman found for his pupils in their composition tests. And these were College Entrance Board Examination candidates.

Before concluding the discussion of these matters, some mention should be made of Wallin's [58] investigation which was taken by many to have successfully refuted the findings of Rice and Cornman. Wallin first described the phenomenal improvement in spelling in the schools of Cleveland, Ohio, in the three years from 1905 to 1908. Following a drill method, which emphasized, (*a*) initial focalization (*b*), attentive repetition, and (*c*) automatic behavior, the teachers taught only two new words a day. The ten new words of one week became the "subordinate" words for review during the next two weeks. Every eighth week oral and written interschool contests were held, the contest words being the eighty words studied during the preceding eight weeks. There were also a series of annual contests. Each word was reviewed four times in two years. On a test given in 1905 the average spelling achievement of the Cleveland schools was 75 per cent; the same test, repeated in 1908, following three years of the drill system yielded an accuracy of 94 per cent.

Wallin's own experiment was conducted in the Cleveland schools after this drill method had been in force several years. The experiment was directed to the end of determining to what extent the learning of words in column dictation would carry over to the situation of spelling the same words when they were written in a dictated composition. This particular question does not concern us here. However, the investigation yields some data relative to spelling efficiency. It was through inferences from these data that Wallin thought he had refuted Rice and Cornman.

The subjects were more than a thousand Cleveland school children who had studied the words of the tests in the manner described above. The children had participated that year in at least one interschool contest in which the test words had been used. The elapsed time between the study of the words and the tests varied among the different classes from three to thirteen weeks. In substance Wallin's tests showed the results obtained from teaching the words by the drill method when measured three to thirteen weeks after study. The general average for all schools participating in the experiment was more than 97 per cent of the words correct. Wallin thought that this percentage revealed a much higher spelling achievement than was shown by Cornman's column tests. However, he is hardly justified in making the comparison because Wallin's subjects were known to have studied recently the words while it is not certain that Cornman's pupils had met the words at all before the test. The comparison is also unreliable because the words were not the same and there was no way of determining the relative difficulty of the words in the two tests. Of course, Wallin's results could not be compared with those of Cornman's composition tests.

The two features which accounted for the success of Wallin's pupils would seem to be the small number of words taught and the strong motivation derived from the interschool contests. Teaching two words a day and allowing time for contests and review would mean about 2,500 words in the elementary curriculum. This is much less than the four or five thousand that many authorities to-day would teach. This question will not be discussed at this point, but will be taken up in connection with the consideration of the experimental data of this study.

Modern teachers would probably not look upon the contest feature as an unmixed blessing. One reads much between the lines in the answers to a questionnaire sent to the participating teachers and principals. Although the drill method had all the prestige that goes with the established system, many of the teachers and principals had the temerity to say that the contests resulted in (1) unfair comparisons, (2) nerve strain, (3) slighting of other branches, (4) unrest, and that there was a doubt that the spelling in composition had been improved. Certainly the modern teacher would distrust this liberal use of contests.

Why is it that the more revolutionary implications of the studies of Rice and Cornman have not been subjected to more thorough-going experimental and statistical analysis? Modern educators may no longer be interested in the old debate over general methods—incidental *vs.* drill. The question of the importance of the learning that goes on outside the regular spelling period was squarely posed and it was important to learn how this incidental learning could be facilitated if it was to rejuvenate old methods. It is difficult to find the report of a major scientific experiment which has followed Cornman's lead in the actual suspension of regular spelling teaching over a period of years. Of course, the time required and the facilities necessary have made such a project prohibitive for most.

Has not spelling research been unduly conservative? The two pioneer investigations mentioned above had great influence on school practice in the first decade of the century. The literature abounds with plaints from laymen and educators about the low estate into which spelling had fallen under the relaxation of drill. But spelling research was not so radically affected. Wallin's work probably grew out of the reaction to incidental teaching. Other studies have not so much questioned the fundamental issue of how spelling is really learned, as they have assumed that a specific spelling period is to be taken for granted and that therefore the pertinent questions were related to specific classroom methods, such as the teaching of homonyms together or apart, the study of words singly or in context, oral or silent study, the value of rules. This is not meant in any sense as a disparagement. Such work was needed and was and is fruitful for it investigates the nature of the learning process in spelling as it goes on in the spelling period. But it would have been valuable if a like energy had been devoted to increasing the knowledge of the conditions of the growth of spelling ability in situations other than those of the spelling period.

Until the studies of Hollingworth and Gates, which have sought to establish fundamental principles, psychological experiments have in the main been barren because the experimental designs and the conclusions sought have been in terms of a highly general and artificially pure or general psychology and have not been translatable into an applied psychology of spelling. In fact, it might be said that they have had little to do with spelling. The psychologists were not interested in spelling, or reading, or arithmetic, etc., but in formulating generalizations and expressing the generalizations in the terminology peculiar to the school to which they belonged. As Gates has indicated, much of this work went forward on the assumption that the form of the mental function was the controlling factor. Therefore, there has been much talk about visual imagery, auditory perception, and the like. The worth of such investigations need not be discussed except to point out that the relation between general and applied psychology does not seem to be as close as that between pure physical science, let us say, and applied physical science. To get "chemically pure" materials, for use in investigating the laws of forgetting, Ebbinghaus had to use nonsense syllables. But nonsense syllables are so alien to the materials of real experience that any principles as to the form of the mental function of forgetting could not possibly hold with meaningful material. Likewise psychological investigations of the general sensory, motor, and associated processes used in spelling have not told much about spelling.

Beginning with Pearson [43] in 1911, educational research in spelling entered a period characterized by more specific problems and more exact scientific methods than those prevalent in the previous decade. Pearson, himself, in his article attempted to formulate some of the principles of more exact research and offered an example in his own experiment in the teaching of homonyms. (It is a tribute to the difficulty of spelling research problems that Finkenbinder [17] in an equally careful experiment came to an almost opposite conclusion.) As the present investigation does not bear on these problems of special method, time will not be taken to discuss them.

During the last ten years two methods that might be termed general have enlisted the partisanship of teachers of spelling. Reference is made to the so-called study-test and test-study methods. Sometimes slightly different forms of the two methods have been described respectively as the group and individual methods.

The test-study procedure has come into such widespread use that its merits to many seem unquestioned. Professor Horn [26] has so aptly stated the principles that support it with particular force that his words are worth quoting:

. . . The indications are that efficiency in teaching spelling is to be increased by a specific attack on the individual words to be learned. This is in line with the whole tendency in modern experimental education, a tendency which has been well outlined by Thorndike in his discussion of education as the formation of specific bonds. In harmony with this point of view the problem of spelling has been attacked; first, by seeking to discover precisely the words which we most frequently need to spell; second, by attempting to grade these words scientifically; third, by attempting to discover the most economical methods of learning them, and fourth by devising means by which progress in learning the words may be measured.

The theoretical superiority of the test-study method has not been realized in several comparative investigations. Keener [33] had 100 words taught to 488 pairs of Chicago school children at the rate of 20 words per week and with an expenditure of fifteen minutes school time per day. The pupils were paired on the basis of an initial spelling test. One group was taught by the group method. The teacher wrote the word on the board, pronounced it, explained the meaning, used it in a sentence, or had pupils do so, spelled it orally, spelled it orally with pupils in concert, pointed out difficult parts, had pupils write the word, spelled it orally while pupils corrected their work, and had each pupil make a personal list of misspelled words. The procedure was repeated for words of general difficulty. At the end of the week the words were tested. The other group was taught by the individual method. On Friday a test of 20 words for the coming week was given. Monday to Thursday each pupil studied the words he missed. The method of individual study was to pronounce the word in a whisper, learn meaning of the word, cover the word and attempt to visualize it while spelling it, then look at the word to see if it was correctly spelled, cover the word again and write it, then compare the written form with the correct form.

His results were inconclusive. In three grades there was a slight difference in favor of the group method; in four, in favor of the individual. For the 488 pairs of pupils in all grades, the superiority of the individual method was 0.7 per cent; in the fourth to eighth grades, the individual method showed a superiority of 1 per cent. The principal advantage to the credit of the individual method was that 12 per cent of the pupils were excused because of perfect scores on the initial test.

Kilzer [34] made up two spelling lists of 25 words each, the words of one list being matched with those of the other according to frequency of use as given by the Commonwealth List and according to difficulty as given by the Ayres Scale. The range of difficulty was from 66 per cent to 88 per cent for eighth grade children. To assure further that the results would not be affected by any variation in the difficulty of the two lists, the subjects were divided into two groups. One group studied the first list by the test-study method and the second by the study-test method. In the other group the arrangement was reversed.

The study-test method was applied thus: The teacher spent five minutes pronouncing the words, each pupil following the pronunciation on a printed list of the words. Then twenty minutes were used in studying the words without help or directions from the teacher. The printed lists were collected and ten minutes given to dictating the words to the pupils who spelled them on blanks provided them. The total time was thirty-five minutes.

Several days later the second list of words was dictated to the same pupils. This took ten minutes. The papers were exchanged and misspellings were marked, the child using a printed list as his guide for the correct spelling. The words misspelled were marked on the printed list and this list handed to the student who had missed the marked words. Then each pupil studied the words he had missed for ten minutes. Again ten minutes was taken for a test. Total time was thirty-five minutes. The latter method was the test-study method.

The tests given immediately after the completion of the study period in each case were termed "immediate recall" tests. Five months later the same pupils were given the same tests. These were termed "delayed recall" tests. The experiment is very incompletely reported. No detailed results are given. Some of the conclusions are: (1) On the immediate recall tests, the chances are 226 to 1 for one group and 80 to 1 for another that the test-study method is superior. (2) On the delayed recall tests there was nothing to choose between the two methods. (3) In 30 per cent of the cases, words correctly spelled on the first test of the

test-study plan were misspelled on the second test. (4) Fifteen
per cent of the pupils misspelled no words on the initial test. (5)
The test-study method saves pupil's time. In so far as it can be
judged from the way the results are reported, there does not seem
to be much to choose between the two methods. At least, after
five months there was no difference.

Of the published investigations relating to the merits of the two
general methods under discussion, the two foregoing are the only
ones that the writer has been able to find which present quantita-
tive data of any validity. Of course there may be many unpublished investigations. It is surprising that such a widely accepted
method as the test-study has not had better experimental verification. There are indications that a merely general comparison of
the efficiency of the two methods is unprofitable. They must be
studied with reference to their comparative worth in dealing with
pupils of different intellectual and educational levels, and with
regard to the number and difficulty of words to be taught. Perhaps a combination of the methods incorporating the strong
features of each may be found to be superior.

Any study of the effectiveness of the teaching of spelling must
be directly concerned with certain curriculum problems which
have to do with the number of words to be taught, the selection
of those words, and their proper grading, for the efficiency of the
teaching will depend in part upon these factors.

Rice's startling disclosures of the apparent lack of relation between the length of the spelling period and spelling achievement,
the need for finding time for the many new subjects demanding a
place in the school program, and the increasing conviction that
the learning of spelling was specific, focused attention of investigators upon the need for determining the most widely and frequently used words in reading and in correspondence and other
writings. The movement bore ripe fruit with the publication of
The Teacher's Word Book by Thorndike and *A Basic Writing
Vocabulary* by Horn. Further studies by Jones [31], French [18],
and Bauer [8] have been more specifically directed to the deter-
mination of children's vocabularies.

Admirable as these lists are for the purposes of research and
teaching, they do not settle the questions of what words and how
many words should be taught. While it would be generally agreed
that the spelling curriculum of the elementary school should

provide for the learning of the 1,000 most commonly used words as given by Horn or Thorndike, and that with few exceptions no words should be included that were outside the 10,000 words of these lists, it is not at all clear that all the words of the second 1,000, the third 1,000, the fourth 1,000 should necessarily be taught. Even in the case of the first 1,000 words of the Commonwealth List some would object to including all because a number of the words relate exclusively to adult experience. In such cases it is argued that words of adults should be replaced with words in children's vocabularies. The disagreement on this score would become more pronounced with the second and third 1,000 words.

An examination of some of the representative spellers makes clear this lack of agreement. The authors of the Breed-French Speller [10] hold that both adult usage and child usage should be considered in selecting words. If words are chosen upon the basis of adult usage, it is said many words are included which are beyond the child's intellectual level and many words at the child's level of experience are excluded. On the other hand, a list made up exclusively of words from children's vocabularies would be inadequate in preparing for adult life. The authors set up the requirement that a word must appear frequently in the written vocabularies of both children and adults, or very frequently in either to be included in their lists. They give in some detail the number of words chosen according to the various criteria:

1. Words used by both children and adults
   (a) appearing in three or more childhood vocabularies 2,298
   (b) appearing in only two childhood vocabularies and having frequencies of 10 or more in the composite adult list 456
   (c) appearing in only one childhood vocabulary and having frequencies of 20 or more in the composite adult list 277
2. Words used by children only and appearing in 3 or more childhood vocabularies 211
3. Words used by adults only and having a frequency of 25 or more in the composite adult list 239
4. Additional words of sufficiently high frequency,
   (a) from French's study of children's letters 23
   (b) from Warning's study of adult correspondence 292
   (c) from the Commonwealth List 44

                                                              3,840
5. Rejected on account of questionable usage 22

                                                              3,818

The primary principle of word selection of the latest Horn-Ashbaugh Speller [27] is that of adult usage. The Commonwealth List is the basic list used. Concerning childish needs, the authors state:

> Comparison of the studies of the speaking and writing vocabularies of children with those of adult vocabulary shows that at any grade level there are available more words than can be used in a spelling course which are of high importance both in the vocabularies of children and in the permanent vocabularies of everyday life. Therefore no word found in studies of child vocabularies has been included in the speller unless it is also found with high frequency in writing done in life outside the school. Thus both childish and permanent needs are met.

In his investigation of the vocabulary of children's themes Jones [31] found 4,532 different words in a total of nearly 15,000,000 running words written. It is interesting to note that 1,927 of these words appeared in the themes of second grade pupils while the average number of different words used per pupil was 521; in the fifth grade there were 3,270 different words used with an average number per pupil of 1,498; in the eighth grade 4,532 different words and an average number per pupil of 2,135.

In his spelling book Jones [32] has followed the principle of selecting words according to child usage as ascertained in his investigation. The 4,532 different words which he found in the children's themes were allotted to grades as follows: There were 524 words used by 50 per cent of the children in the second grade, 625 words by 40 per cent of the children in the third grade, 754 words by 30 per cent of the children in the fourth grade, 769 words by 20 per cent of the children in the fifth grade, 750 words by 20 per cent of the children in the sixth grade, 578 words by 15 per cent of the children in the seventh grade, and 502 words by 10 per cent of the children in the eighth grade.

The source for the words of the Thorndike-Wohlfarth [51] spelling book was in the main the first 3,000 of the Thorndike List. The authors found that, ". . . with comparatively few exceptions the first three thousand words of the Thorndike List correspond closely with the children's writing vocabularies." [52] When the first 3,000 of the Thorndike List were checked against the Commonwealth List, a "high degree of correspondence" appeared, but there were many words that were not common.

Instances could be multiplied to illustrate the point that there is far from substantial agreement among leading authorities upon either the specific words to be taught in the elementary school or principles to be used in their selection.

At this point, it may be suggested that the concept of the "most commonly used words" involves many difficulties. Sociologically, no doubt it should be possible to determine the 5,000 or 10,000 most commonly used words for a social group or even a nation. But there is also a psychological aspect to the matter. Would the individual variation in the use of words by members of the group be so small that each individual list of "most commonly used words" would substantially agree with each of the other individual lists? Would the lists, say of 75 per cent of the members of a group, be substantially the same?

Ayres [6] found it impossible in his investigation to identify the 2,000 most commonly used words. He concluded that only 1,000 words at the outside could be so termed. His study is too well known to need detailing. He analyzed about 368,000 words written by 2,500 persons and discovered that nine-tenths of the words were found in the first 1,000. The more extensive later investigations have tended to verify his conclusion.

Horn expresses his idea in the following words:

> After a thousand words are taught, the addition of each group of approximately 1,000 words adds a very small percentage to the number of running words which can be spelled by the learner. The learning of words beyond the fourth thousand in frequency adds only about one per cent to the number of running words the pupil can control.

When the wide range of material which Horn used to compile the Commonwealth List is considered and when it seems probable that the great majority of pupils will not need to write more than two or three different types of material, the probability that one individual's list of most frequently used words beyond the first 1,000 will approximate another's must be taken as remote. Of course, the inclusion of so many different sorts of written materials for compilation makes for sociological validity of Horn's list. On the other hand, the fact that it was necessary to use so many different kinds of writing to get a valid list indicates that the list cannot be an individual one.

Cook and O'Shea [15] examined the correspondence of thirteen persons. The examination of about 200,000 running words yielded a total of 5,200 different words. Only 186 words were used by all thirteen correspondents, only 577 different words were used by a majority of the thirteen, and there were 2,230 words which were used by not more than one of the thirteen. Jones [31] found that the children of the second grade used more than 1,900 words in themes, but the average number of words per pupil was only 521. These studies indicate the wide variability in the vocabularies of both children and adults.

It does not seem improbable that a list of words which purported to be a list of the 2,000, 3,000, or 4,000 most commonly used words in writing would have to be compiled from the writing of a group, homogeneous in vocational and social status, and such a list would be valid only for individuals of the defined group. Perhaps the evidence still does not justify such a broad generalization. However, it does seem certain that there is no agreement among those best entitled to an opinion as to what words or how many words should be taught in the elementary school. The words of the spelling curriculum must be selected from the best vocabulary studies, but what words and the number of words to be taught remain to be determined.

Pending the resolution of these uncertainties, it may be suggested that another aspect of the situation has not received the attention which it deserves. To what extent should the initial difficulty or pre-study difficulty of words, the learning difficulty of words, and the permanence of learning be taken into account in making the curriculum in spelling? It is a principle of curriculum construction that the school should not spend its energies upon activities that are already adequately cared for by other social institutions.

If this principle is sound, it should be desirable to know whether or not there is a substantial number of words that can safely be left to be learned through reading and other verbal experiences. If a substantial number of such words could be identified, it should then be in order to institute inquiries as to the learning difficulties of words of various usages and frequencies with a view to determining whether or not the importance of a word as judged by range and frequency of usage warrants the effort necessary for the elementary school child to master it. Present practices do not seem to consider ease or difficulty of learning in the selection of words to be taught. In consequence there is a wide variance of opinion as to the number of words which can be thoroughly taught.

The number of words that can be effectively taught should influence the way in which we use the vocabulary lists in making the curriculum.

The difficulty of words has been used by some authorities as a partial basis for the grade placement of words. Others employ it only to equalize the daily lesson load. What might be called the learning difficulty of a word, that is, the amount of time and effort to master the word when its spelling is not known, is not always distinguished from what might be called the initial difficulty of the word—the difficulty as determined by the percentage of pupils who cannot spell it before study. Horn [26], who grades his words in part on the basis of difficulty, says, "The frequency with which a given word is misspelled in a given grade does not necessarily indicate under present conditions the difficulty of learning that word."

It seems to be assumed by many that when a large number of children in a grade misspell a word before studying it, the word should be placed in a higher grade. In such cases it is inferred that the initial difficulty correlates highly with the learning difficulty. Experimental investigation may find a low instead of a high correlation.

The foregoing paragraphs have presented some aspects of the general spelling situation that are still a source of uncertainty and perplexity, and that should be kept in mind throughout any consideration of the general effectiveness of spelling instruction. In summary, it may be said that the investigations discussed have implied the significance of the following matters:

1. The learning of the spelling period must be considered in its relation to the learnings of spelling that are ancillary or incidental to the learning of reading, writing, and other school subjects. May some words be left to incidental learning, in view of the many demands upon the spelling period, and in view of its limited efficiency?

2. The habit of correctly spelling what one writes in and out of school is not the same thing as the ability to spell words correctly when they are dictated in the spelling period, or at some later time. This fact should be borne in mind in setting up standards for evaluating the work in spelling. It probably accounts in part for the apparently contradictory results achieved by Rice and Cornman, on the one hand, and Wallin, on the other.

The uncertain validity of school methods of measuring results must always be kept in mind.

3. It has been too readily assumed that the test-study method is definitely superior to the study-test procedure. This assumption has in turn tended to instill a complacency that is blind to existing deficiencies in spelling achievements. The question of the best general method is not yet a closed one.

4. What is prescribed for the curriculum upon sociological and philosophical considerations must always be limited by what can actually be accomplished in the schoolroom, The questions of the number of words to be taught specifically, and the particular words to be selected have not yet been answered satisfactorily.

CHAPTER II

THE PROBLEM AND THE CONDITIONS OF THE EXPERIMENT

STATEMENT OF THE PROBLEM

How effectively does a daily spelling period of fifteen minutes provide the children with relatively permanent habits of correct spelling of the words taught, assuming a school reaching or exceeding the norms for the country at large in all branches of its instruction, and employing methods formulated and carried out in the light of the best scientific knowledge?

The plan was to carry out the investigation under actual school conditions. No special incentives such as drives for better spelling, or contests, were to be employed. All that the teachers were to know about the matter was that special records were being kept. All the words usually taught were to be taught during the term so that there would be no temptation to stress "test" words. Permanent learning was to be measured by a test given six months after teaching with a summer vacation included in the six months period.

Under these conditions some of the more special problems were:

1. How well can children spell the words assigned to the grade before they study them?
   A. When the pupils of a grade are sectioned on the basis of general intelligence, educational achievement, and teachers' estimates, how do the respective groups compare in ability to spell the words before study and after study?
2. To what extent does the order of difficulty of words on an initial or pre-study test continue to be the order of difficulty upon a test given six months after teaching the words and designed to measure the permanence of the learning?
   A. Do words of approximately the same initial difficulty fall into distinct groups characterized by different degrees of "learning difficulty," that is, are some very hard to learn

22

although of about equal pre-study difficulty and others very easy?

3. How do the various ability groups of children compare as to permanence of learning?

4. How should the improvement that takes place as a result of study be evaluated? How should it be measured to justify the statement that the learning has been efficient, moderately efficient, or inefficient?

A. What does the degree of learning efficiency found imply as to methods of teaching, the number of words to be taught, and the grade placement of words?

DESCRIPTION OF THE INVESTIGATION

The School

The data were procured in an elementary school situated in Brooklyn, New York, and having an enrollment of about 1,800 pupils. The school serves a residential district which might be described as lower middle class. No extremes of wealth or poverty are represented. The children are clean, well fed, and well kept. The writer was impressed by their good manners, which were probably more a product of school than of home training. The school population would not differ in economic and social position from a typical group of any of the larger cities of the country except that it has a rather high percentage of Jewish pupils.

Judged by the methods of instruction employed, the school would probably be termed a conventional one. It is well organized and an observer at once senses that the morale of the school is high. Although conventional in type, it must not be implied that it is not progressive. The best evidence of this is that the principal has enthusiastically coöperated for a number of years with members of the faculty of Teachers College in carrying on extensive investigations in reading, spelling, and other studies. The principal has cheerfully shouldered the burden of keeping accurate and extensive records of much experimental work and has always been ready to experiment.

Of the ten or twelve schools of the district, this school easily ranks among the first three in all respects and is the leader in many. An elaborate system of classification of pupils is in effect. Each child is graded and classified upon the basis of group intelligence tests when he enters. At regular periods additional ratings according to group intelligence tests, achievement tests, and teachers' estimates are compiled and each child is regarded and reclassified according to the ratings. At least three differentiations are made in the classes of a half-grade and sometimes there are as many as five sections in a half-grade when the number of pupils warrants.

No intelligence or achievement tests were given in connection with this investigation. The ratings and grading of the children as already made were followed. However, the writer inspected the results of many of the intelligence and achievement examinations. At every grade level the achievement equaled or exceeded the norms for the country as a whole with respect to general intelligence. On the Stanford Achievement Test the norms of each grade equaled those for the country at large in all subjects except those of nature study and science.

The Method of Teaching Spelling

The observations were made under ordinary school conditions. The teachers did not know that any specific experiment was going on, or how the records which they turned in were to be used. They were only aware that the principal was making a school-wide investigation of spelling. Most of them had in previous terms participated in like studies of reading and knew from this experience that their efficiency as teachers was not in question.

The method of teaching spelling in use throughout the school was the well known test-study method. The week's work was mapped out in the following fashion: On Monday, a pre-study test of all the new words for the week was given. The teacher pronounced the word, used it in a sentence, and explained the meaning when necessary. The child wrote the word. No alteration of the first spelling was permitted. Words were corrected by the children and then checked later by the teacher. Any word altered or illegible was counted wrong. Before the period ended each child entered his misspelled words in correct form on an individual list labeled "Spelling Demons." This list was used for further study. Tuesday was given up to the individual study of the words missed on Monday. The instructions for this individual study were as follows:

(a) Require pupils to pronounce words carefully, distinctly, enunciating each syllable and looking closely at the syllable as it is said.

(b) With closed eyes try to see the word syllable by syllable as it is pronounced in a whisper. Try to recall how the word looked and at the the same time say the letters. Spell by syllables.

(c) Open eyes and look at the word. If you do not have it right, go over (a) and (b) above. Keep trying until you can say the letters correctly with closed eyes.

(d) When you are sure that you have learned the word, write it and then compare. If you fail, do steps (a), (b), and (c) again.

(e) Write the word again. See if it is right. If it is right, do it again and compare. Now try to write it a third time. The word is learned when it is written correctly on three successive writings.

The teacher should closely supervise the pupil's study to insure that pupils work aggressively and that proper methods of learning are used. She should utilize this opportunity to investigate the study methods of children who have shown unsatisfactory results in the final test of the preceding week and to correct wrong habits where such are found to have developed. The Friday tests provide an unfailing index of efficiency. When any pupil makes a poor record on a Friday test, the teacher should inspect his methods of study on the following Tuesday in order to determine and remove the cause of the trouble. While the class as a whole should not be tested on Tuesday, the teacher may test individual pupils to see how effectively they have studied.

On Wednesday a second test of the words for the week was given. Thursday was given over to individual study of the words missed on Wednesday, and if there were time, to words previously missed or to review words. A third test was given Friday. Each pupil made a record of the words he missed on this test, and they were carried over to the next week for further study. The teachers were encouraged to attempt to develop pride in correct spelling and it was suggested to them that interest might be fostered through class and individual graphs, by encouraging the pupils to use the words studied in other written work and through occasional spelling matches. Pupils who correctly spelled all the words on the Monday test were excused from the spelling class for the week, but they were required to take the Friday test.

Every fourth week was given up to review work. The same procedures were followed, but the words were review words. For this investigation the records for this work were not available.

The Data

Initial Tests. For each week except the fourth the teacher of each room in all grades from the second to the eighth made a report for the 20 words of the week. This report showed the number of pupils missing each word on the Monday or pre-study test, the percentage of correct spellings for each word, and the number of pupils spelling the word. At the top of each list information was given as to the name of the teacher, the date, and the classification of the pupils. The same lists of words were used in each room of the half-grade each week regardless of whether or not the pupils belonged to slow, average, or fast groups. From the reports made by the teacher, there was compiled a consolidated list for the whole half-grade. This consolidated list provided a record showing the percentage of correct spellings for each word for each ability group and the percentage of correct spellings for the half-grade as a whole.

For convenience, the Monday or pre-study tests given during the spring term of 1928 are hereafter regarded as parts of a single test and are referred to collectively as the initial tests or Test 1. The reader must not be led to think that they were special tests. The tests were an integral part of the method in use.

Retention Tests. The words taught during the spring term of 1928 were arranged in tests of 50 words each. The order of the words in the tests was the same as that in which they had been taught. During the fourth week of school in the fall term of 1928, the first test of 50 words was dictated to the same general group of pupils who had taken the initial test on the words and studied them during the spring term of 1928. The second test of 50 words was given during the eighth week of school and every fourth week thereafter a test of 50 words was given until all the words taught in the spring of 1928 had been tested again. The arrangement of the tests was such that each word was tested a second time about six months after it had been taught. These second tests are collectively referred to hereafter as the retention tests or Test 2. Throughout the term regular spelling instruction in new words went on, and no special instruction was given in connection with the words appearing in the retention tests.

The group of pupils was not exactly the same because some pupils had not progressed and others had not returned to school. The number who dropped out in this manner averaged about 10 per cent in each half-grade. The composition of the slow, normal, and fast groups also underwent some changes due to reclassification. For example, in Grade 7A there were five sections during the spring term of 1928. On account of withdrawal and non-promotion the number of sections was reduced to four when the 7B classes were organized in the fall of 1929. The pupils of 7A5 were distributed among the other sections according to ability. Were this investigation a laboratory one in which the effect of the change in one variable was being measured, these displacements might cloud the issue. This investigation seeks only to show what happens as a result of spelling instruction under actual school conditions. The changes in the school population and the rearrangements due to reclassification operated with respect to all the words in approximately the same degree. If a word shows a greater gain in percentage of correct spellings from the spring of 1928 to the fall of 1929 than another, it could hardly be due to the fact that the group who spelled the word in the fall of 1928 had changed more than the group who spelled the other word. In those cases where a shift in the school population was so great as to seriously invalidate any conclusions based on the assumption that the groups were the same, the words were not included.

Number of Words and Number of Pupils

Table 3 gives the number of words in each half-grade for which there are complete records for both the initial and retention tests,

TABLE 3
NUMBER OF WORDS AND NUMBER OF PUPILS FOR WHICH THERE ARE COMPLETE RECORDS

GRADE	NUMBER OF WORDS	NUMBER OF PUPILS
2A	98	110
2B	125	154
3A	235	101
3B	172	141
4A	115	108
4B	151	96
5A	229	176
5B	90	86
6A	169	83
6B	232	120
7A	250	126
7B	114	128
8A	147	99
Total	2,127	1,528

and the number of pupils spelling the word in both tests. In Grade 2A, for example, there were only 98 words for which there were complete records, and the number of pupils spelling these words on both tests was 110. All the data except that relating to fast, slow, and average groups and certain data marked "supplementary" are based on the number of words and the number of pupils shown in Table 3. The data for the fast and slow groups are based on only about 30 spellings per word.

Frequency of Use of the Words

Table 4 gives the distribution of the words according to the Thorndike List [49]. It reads as follows: In Grade 2 there were 138 words belonging to the first half of the first 1,000, 38 words in the second half of the first 1,000, 11 words in the first half of the second 1,000, etc.

TABLE 4 *

DISTRIBUTION OF WORDS ACCORDING TO POSITION IN THORNDIKE LIST

	GRADE 2	GRADE 3	GRADE 4	GRADE 5	GRADE 6	GRADE 7	GRADE 8	TOTAL
1a	138	155	23	14	4	1	1	336
1b	38	97	55	52	17	1	0	260
2a	11	53	47	45	42	24	3	225
2b	9	24	30	51	41	25	4	184
3a	1	14	24	20	52	41	2	154
3b	0	8	22	19	38	39	7	133
4a	1	1	10	13	33	35	8	101
4b	0	3	7	11	18	24	7	70
5a	2	4	23	27	73	123	73	325
Total ..	200	359	241	252	318	313	105	1,788

* *Note:* There were 339 words not found in the Thorndike List. Many of them were simple derivatives which are not listed separately in that list.

Spelling Ability of the Pupils as Measured by the Iowa Spelling Scales

In Table 5 the percentages of correct spellings for 20 words in each grade on the initial tests are compared with the percentages given in the Iowa Spelling Scales for the same grade. The 20 words were selected at random from the words of the initial tests, except that 10 words were chosen from the lower half of the grade and

TABLE 5

LISTS OF RANDOMLY SELECTED WORDS WITH PERCENTAGE OF CORRECT SPELL-
INGS ACCORDING TO THE IOWA SPELLING SCALE AND INITIAL TESTS

WORD	IOWA SCALE Percentage Correct	INITIAL TEST Percentage Correct	WORD	IOWA SCALE Percentage Correct	INITIAL TEST Percentage Correct
Grade 2			Grade 3		
away	77	64	above	52	61
both	43	62	beside	69	83
card	44	71	coming	66	52
cow	76	71	does	50	50
eat	72	71	every	75	62
get	76	66	fix	57	48
grass	64	56	Friday	75	57
like	68	82	ground	69	56
more	43	60	talk	65	69
my	87	66	only	59	48
now	63	80	pack	64	64
pay	58	55	state	77	87
said	53	43	weak	62	63
seem	41	63	peach	64	81
so	82	91	meat	83	92
that	83	45	date	71	94
time	70	66	filling	57	66
top	68	63	board	44	47
very	50	69	below	68	85
wall	63	68	read	80	85
Average	64	66	Average	65	67
Grade 4			Grade 5		
able	88	97	account	66	62
between	80	65	company	84	89
clothing	81	75	extra	77	78
cotton	74	54	however	98	94
farmer	86	87	known	74	74
herself	74	84	postal	79	59
lump	83	86	rate	90	83
people	90	88	score	78	87
raw	68	55	stranger	89	87
wheel	87	63	wedding	82	89
action	51	68	advance	81	82
contest	81	94	closely..........	65	75
exchange	59	80	extend..........	79	81
honest..........	57	86	hospital.........	72	71
lonesome	60	85	neglect	70	69
moment	71	81	remark	90	95
newspaper	75	88	safety	51	63
perfect	69	72	signed	57	65
seventh	78	90	local	75	75
Thursday	78	78	collect	64	98
Average	74	79	Average	77	79

TABLE 5 (*Continued*)

WORD	IOWA SCALE Percentage Correct	INITIAL TEST Percentage Correct	WORD	IOWA SCALE Percentage Correct	INITIAL TEST Percentage Correct
	Grade 6			Grade 7	
absence	71	56	accomplish	82	75
certain	76	81	consideration	87	85
continue	90	78	expense	75	81
decline	84	79	issue	86	92
direct	90	89	patent	84	65
earnest	90	81	represent	86	91
foundation	82	81	succeed	66	70
guide	81	82	receipt	48	38
humor	78	69	universal	80	75
magazine	55	50	vicinity	73	62
author	92	63	accordance	72	73
constant	79	84	Christian	75	59
favorable	79	85	unusual	65	80
linen	85	77	straightened	54	81
popular	76	90	necessary	49	55
reliable	87	73	merit	53	96
quoted	86	82	same	59	88
seldom	79	90	organization	60	77
series	57	74	community	53	79
volume	79	68	congratulate	63	55
Average	80	77	Average	69	74

10 from the upper half. This was done to make the percentages obtained from the experimental school comparable to those of the Iowa Scale as the percentages given in that scale are for the middle of the year. The experimental school seems to be slightly superior in spelling ability, according to this scale, in Grades 2, 3, and 5; substantially superior in Grades 4 and 7; and somewhat inferior in Grade 6. The superiority of the experimental school is possibly greater than the figures reveal for the reason that it is known that the children of this school had not studied the words. In the case of the words of the Iowa Scales, it is not known whether or not some of the children had had an opportunity to study the words at some time in their school career.

A SIMPLE STATISTICAL REPRESENTATION OF THE DATA

The Initial Tests

In Tables 6, 7, and 8 the quartile distribution of the percentages of correct spellings for the 2,127 words of the investigation is shown for each half-grade as a whole, and for the fast and slow classes. Table 6 reads as follows: In Grade 2A, 25 per cent of the words were spelled with an accuracy of 57 per cent or less; 50 per cent with an accuracy of 66 per cent or less; and 75 per cent with an accuracy of 76 per cent or less. Taking all the half-grades together, 25 per cent of the words were spelled correctly by 65 per cent of the pupils or less; 50 per cent of the words by 76 per cent or less; and 75 per cent by 84 per cent or less. In connection with the fast classes, it is significant that 25 per cent of the words were spelled with an accuracy of 94 per cent or better by the pupils of these classes.

TABLE 6

QUARTILE DISTRIBUTION OF PERCENTAGES OF CORRECT
SPELLINGS ON INITIAL TEST

GRADE	Q_1	Md.	Q_3
2A	57%	66%	76%
2B	62	69	78
3A	52	64	71
3B	58	68	76
4A	71	80	88
4B	74	82	88
5A	71	79	86
5B	70	77	83
6A	69	79	86
6B	65	76	87
7A	65	75	88
7B	66	76	84
8A	61	72	81
Median	65%	76%	84%

TABLE 7

QUARTILE DISTRIBUTION OF PERCENTAGES OF CORRECT SPELLINGS ON INITIAL TEST—RAPID SECTIONS

GRADE	Q₁	Md.	Q₃
2A	74%	82%	91%
2B	84	92	97
3A	81	90	97
3B	81	87	94
4A	71	83	89
4B	81	89	93
5A	79	86	94
5B	79	87	93
6A	67	79	87
6B	67	81	91
7A	69	83	94
7B	80	88	95
8A	77	89	94
Median	79%	87%	94%

TABLE 8

DATA OF TABLE 7 FOR SLOW SECTIONS

GRADE	Q₁	Md.	Q₃
2A	60%	71%	84%
2B	19	32	44
3A	29	42	52
3B	39	52	65
4A	59	69	80
4B	57	74	85
5A	43	56	69
5B	48	63	76
6A	58	67	79
6B	55	68	81
7A	73	82	91
7B	53	67	78
8A	52	66	75
Median	53%	67%	78%

The Retention Tests

Tables 9, 10, and 11 give the median percentages correct and the quartile distribution of the percentages correct for the various grades for the retention tests. The retention tests, it will be remembered, measured the spelling ability of the pupils on the words that had been taught to the same pupils approximately six months previously. Thus it is thought that the retention tests reflect the initial ability on the words plus the permanent gains that may be attributed to the specific teaching and plus any further gain due to the six month's greater maturity of the pupils.

Table 9 gives the figures for each grade as a whole; Table 10 for the rapid sections, and Table 11 for the slow sections. It is of some interest to note that the median and quartile points for the slow sections fall just about as far below the grade median and quartile points as the median and quartile points of the fast sections rise above them.

TABLE 9

QUARTILE DISTRIBUTION OF PERCENTAGES CORRECT ON
RETENTION TEST

GRADE	Q_1	Md.	Q_3
2A	68%	82%	90%
2B	77	83	90
3A	77	83	90
3B	78	84	92
4A	91	95	97
4B	81	89	93
5A	88	92	95
5B	82	89	94
6A	80	86	94
6B	83	90	94
7A	75	85	93
7B	76	86	92
8A	77	84	89
Median	78%	86%	93%

TABLE 10

Quartile Distribution of Percentages Correct on Retention Test—Rapid Sections

Grade	Q₁	Md.	Q₃
2A	92%	97%	100%
2B	95	97	100
3A	92	95	98
3B	78	88	95
4A	92	97	100
4B	86	94	97
5A	87	93	97
5B	83	88	95
6A	82	91	97
6B	96	100	100
7A	85	93	97
7B	88	94	100
8A	84	93	97
Median	87	94	97%

TABLE 11

Data of Table 10 for Slow Sections

Grade	Q₁	Md.	Q₃
2A	37%	63%	81%
2B	53	72	86
3A	56	68	78
3B	59	74	85
4A	85	90	93
4B	74	86	94
5A	83	90	97
5B	72	82	89
6A	70	82	93
6B	75	87	94
7A	63	78	89
7B	67	79	94
8A	67	76	84
Median	67%	79%	89%

Improvement from Initial Tests to Retention Tests

Tables 12, 13, and 14 present the figures which show the median percentage gains and the quartile distribution of the percentage gains for the various grades and ability groups from the initial to the retention tests. It is significant to note that the slow sections show the greatest absolute gains in percentage correct from the first to the second tests. Of course, because of the relatively low percentages of correct spellings on the initial tests the possibilities of gain were great. This raises the question of whether or not the words placed in a given grade should not be considerably harder.

As shown previously in Table 7 the median percentage of correct spellings for the rapid groups was 87 per cent. Consequently it is not surprising that the rapid sections made only an absolute median gain of 6 per cent, while the slow sections made a median gain of 15 per cent. Some aspects of this matter will be referred to later.

TABLE 12

DISTRIBUTION OF PERCENTAGE GAIN—INITIAL TEST TO RETENTION TEST

GRADE	Q_1	Md.	Q_3
2A	8%	15%	22%
2B	9	14	20
3A	15	21	27
3B	11	17	22
4A	8	19	21
4B	1	6	9
5A	8	13	19
5B	5	10	15
6A	3	10	16
6B	7	15	22
7A	4	8	14
7B	5	9	15
8A	5	10	16
Median	7%	13%	19%

TABLE 13

Grade	Q_1	Md.	Q_3
2A	7%	12%	19%
2B	1	4	10
3A	1	6	13
3B	− 6	3	10
4A	8	13	23
4B	0	3	12
5A	1	6	13
5B	− 5	2	9
6A	3	12	20
6B	8	17	32
7A	1	6	20
7B	1	5	12
8A	1	5	14
Median	1%	6%	13%

TABLE 14

Data of Table 13 for Slow Sections

Grade	Q_1	Md.	Q_3
2A	− 32%	− 8%	9%
2B	26	38	48
3A	12	25	34
3B	10	21	32
4A	9	22	30
4B	3	11	21
5A	22	33	44
5B	8	16	28
6A	4	13	22
6B	6	15	28
7A	− 14	− 5	2
7B	3	12	25
8A	1	11	23
Median	6%	15%	28%

Supplementary Data Pertaining to Method and Evaluation

In Table 15 there are presented some supplementary data which give information as to the efficiency of the learning in spelling five weeks after the words were taught. The data were gathered in connection with an investigation of the relative merits of the test-study and the study-test plans of teaching spelling.

The figures refer to the percentage of correct spellings for 100 words which were taught to all pupils in all grades during the spring of 1929. The number of pupils for whom there were complete records for the two tests is given in the first column of Table 15. The table gives the average percentage of correct spellings for the 100 words on an initial test before study and the percentage of correct spellings for the same words and the same group of

TABLE 15

AVERAGE PERCENTAGES CORRECT FOR 100 WORDS ON AN INITIAL TEST, A TEST ABOUT FIVE WEEKS AFTER STUDY AND GAINS FROM TEST TO TEST—FEBRUARY TO APRIL, 1929

GRADE	NUMBER OF PUPILS	INITIAL PERCENTAGE CORRECT	PERCENTAGE CORRECT SECOND TEST	GAIN IN PERCENTAGE CORRECT
2A	127	33%	75%	42%
2B	125	50	82	32
3A	140	50	84	34
3B	164	64	89	25
4A	128	64	90	26
4B	138	68	92	24
5A	62	69	91	22
5B	159	69	95	26
6A	185	73	95	22
6B	83	70	93	23
7A	140	73	92	19
7B	136	71	93	22
8A	123	69	92	23
8B	138	64	94	30
Mean	131	63%	90%	27%

pupils measured five weeks after the words had been taught. For all grades the average improvement was 27 per cent in correct spellings—that is, from an initial average of 63 per cent to an average of 90 per cent on the test five weeks after study. The data for these 100 words supply information missing from the other data—information relative to the level of spelling achievement a short time after the teaching was completed. The 100 words used for this experiment were selected from the regular school curriculum, the same source as the words used in the chief part of this investigation. The tests, however, were not conducted until the spring of 1929, one year after the initial tests of the main experiment. The two experiments were distinct.

CHAPTER III

ANALYSIS AND EVALUATION OF THE DATA

PROBLEM OF EVALUATION OF THE GAINS IN SPELLING ABILITY FROM THE INITIAL TO THE RETENTION TEST

As the figures for the initial tests demonstrate, most words which are graded according to present practices are correctly spelled by upwards of 50 per cent of the pupils before they are given particular attention in the spelling period. Many words are spelled correctly by 90 per cent or more of the pupils before special study.

An ideal way of estimating the worth of the gains due to special study of words in a period set aside for that purpose would be to compare the improvement obtained in this fashion with the improvement that could be expected to take place merely as a function of maturity and incidental learning. Unfortunately, data sufficiently extensive to be reliable and useful in making such comparison do not seem to be in print.

Richards [46] at the San Francisco State Normal School found that in the case of 78 children who were tested with the Ayres Scale and then retested a year later without having any spelling instruction during the year, 67.5 per cent of the children had improved more than one year in spelling ability; 20.4 per cent had remained stationary; and 12 per cent had failed to attain their scores of the year before. Now the Ayres Scale is so constructed that at the time the tests from which it was derived were given, some of the words in some of the grades had been specifically studied and some had not. For example, it is not known what words of Column L had been studied and what words had not been studied before the tests were given, for instance in the fourth grade. The norm for the words of this column in this grade (88 per cent) is based, in part, on words that had been previously studied during the school career of some of the children and words which had not been so studied by a number of the children. The performance of 67 per cent of Richard's pupils must be somewhat

39

better than even the figures show, if specific teaching of spelling has any value.

The Ayres Scale at various points must incorporate the results of unknown amounts of specific instruction. Ballou [7] strongly criticised it on this basis and argued that it could not be used to measure "spelling growth." Other scales share the same limitation. To make a scale that would be capable of adequately measuring "spelling growth," it would be necessary to have a large number of schools with a population sufficient to supply a representative sampling dispense with spelling instruction over a period of eight years and then at the end of the period proceed to construct a scale on the plan of the Iowa Spelling Scales. Lacking such a scale, comparisons of the kind under discussion should be interpreted cautiously.

Before comparing gains shown by this investigation with the gains which the spelling scales reveal, it will be instructive to report an experiment by a very competent investigator which parallels the present study in many ways and to discuss the methods of evaluation there used.

INVESTIGATION BY WOODY AND HIS CONCLUSIONS RELATIVE TO THE PERMANENT EFFECTS OF THE TEACHING OF SPELLING

The fact that certain spelling tests given in the early fall of the year in numerous Michigan cities had revealed a spelling achievement much below the Ayres standards, while tests given in May had indicated an approximation of these standards, led Woody [61] to investigate the permanent effects of teaching.

An extensive investigation was conducted during the second term of the school year 1922–23. The subjects were pupils in the fourth, fifth, and sixth grades in 15 different cities. Four lists of 20 words of each grade were so selected from the Horn-Ashbaugh Spelling Scales that the initial percentages of correct spellings to be expected on the words of List 1 were about 73 per cent; List 2, 66 per cent; List 3, 58 per cent; List 4, 50 per cent.

A pre-study or initial test, Test 1, was followed by the teaching of the words according to the methods commonly employed by the respective teachers who participated in the work. The words were taught until the teacher felt that the 80 words contained in the set of 4 lists had been mastered. A second test, Test 2, was conducted immediately after the completion of the teaching, and a third test, Test 3, one month later. Test 3 occurred near the close of the school year and Test 4 was applied in September following the summer vacation. The words making up the list were not studied after the giving of Test 2. Regular spelling instruction on other words was continued. Thus each grade was tested four times on lists of words of varying difficulty, the last test occurring five or six months after the first.

Woody reports his results in detail for each city, but here only averages of all results will be presented:

TABLE 16

SUMMARY OF THE RESULTS OF WOODY'S INVESTIGATION

GRADE	NUMBER OF PUPILS	PERCENTAGE OF ACCURACY			
		Test 1	Test 2	Test 3	Test 4
		List 1			
4	661	74	96	91	85
5	636	59	95	91	90
6	488	72	97	94	90
		List 2			
4	661	62	94	90	82
5	636	54	92	87	77
6	488	62	96	92	86
		List 3			
4	661	47	89	82	72
5	636	48	91	83	72
6	488	52	92	88	80
		List 4			
4	661	32	86	77	65
5	636	39	89	79	65
6	488	41	93	87	73

Table 16 reads as follows: In Grade 4, 661 pupils spelled the 20 words of List 1 with an accuracy of 74 per cent on the initial test; an accuracy of 96 per cent immediately after study, etc. Grouping together the four lists for each grade, the results for the 80 words taught in each grade are given in Table 17.

TABLE 17

Woody's Results Evaluated in Terms of Equivalent Gain on Ayres Scale and in Terms of the Learning Ratio

GRADE	PERCENTAGES					EQUIVALENT GAIN BY MONTHS, AYRES SCALES	LEARNING RATIOS
	Test 1	Test 2	Test 3	Test 4	Gain Test 1–4		
4	54	91	85	76	22	18	.48
5	50	92	85	76	26	21	.52
6	57	95	90	82	25	28	.58
Average	54	93	87	78	24	21	.52

Woody's purpose was to discover the permanent results of the teaching of spelling. His conclusions in this respect are interesting for the data seem to be susceptible to a radically different interpretation. In his summary he says, "The permanent effect of the teaching of these words was rather surprising. On List 1, the loss between Tests 2 and 3 was from 3 to 5 per cent, and between Tests 3 and 4 from 1 to 6 per cent; . . . on List 4, between Tests 2 and 3 from 6 to 10 per cent and between Tests 3 and 4, from 12 to 15 per cent." In other places he emphasizes the high scores on Test 3 and the fact that losses from Test 2 to Test 3 and from Test 3 to Test 4 are not proportionate to the magnitude of the percentages of correct spellings on the initial tests. Thus, one word may be spelled on the initial tests by 40 per cent or less of the pupils, but it will only go back about 10 per cent in correct spellings from Test 2 to Test 3, whereas the easy word may go back 5 per cent from Test 2 to Test 3.

It is true that the losses from test to test seem very small. In the fourth grade for the words of List 1 the loss from Test 2 to Test 3 is only 5 per cent and from Test 3 to Test 4 only 6 per cent. But the total loss from Test 2 to Test 4 is 11 per cent and that is equal to the total gain from Test 1 to Test 4. That is, after a summer vacation, the words of this list had lost one-half of the gains they had made when measured immediately after study. A business that fixed attention only on the larger expenditures and disregarded the smaller ones might well get into difficulty. And in spelling, it is not clear that small decreases from test to test can be disregarded.

When the gains from Test 1 to Test 4 are compared with the gains shown by words of apparently equal difficulty in the Ayres Scale, the permanent effects of teaching seem to be substantial. If the reader will turn to Table 17 again he will note that 54 per cent was the initial percentage of correct spellings for all the 80 words for the fourth grade and that six months after the teaching of the words, it was increased to 76 per cent—a gain of 22 per cent. The words of Columns Q and R of the Ayres Scale are approximately of 54 per cent average difficulty for the fourth grade. A gain of 22 per cent for these words would be approximately equivalent to a gain of 18 months. (This is based on the assumption that the gain in spelling ability is constant and linear. This assumption is of course only true in a very general way.) Calculated on this basis, the average equivalent gain on the Ayres Scale for the 240 words taught in Woody's experiment is 21 months. As the interval between Test 1 and Test 4 was about 6 months, it would seem that specific teaching could claim credit for bringing about a gain of 15 months more than the normal expectation.

However, certain features of the procedure lead one to suspect that this evaluation of the gain is a rather liberal one. The instructions to the teachers permitted, and in fact actually encouraged, a degree of overlearning that would not be typical under ordinary teaching conditions. The teachers were instructed to teach the words until they had been "mastered." No time limit was set. Under normal school conditions 20 words perhaps are allotted for the week's study. The next week the class begins to study on another group of 20 words, although some of the first 20 words may be carried over for review. In the circumstances of Woody's experiment, the teacher was privileged to keep on teaching the words until they were mastered. Other favorable influences noted by the author were: (1) "The best and most progressive teachers took part in the investigation," (2) " . . . that better results are obtained when teachers are participating

in investigations in which results are frequently measured," (3)
". . . that the teachers participating in this investigation taught
on a much higher plane than usual." In short, there are so many
incalculable and imponderable factors in such comparisons as
have just been made that conclusions must be taken very cautiously.

ANOTHER APPROACH TO THE PROBLEM OF EVALUATION OF SPELLING GAINS

Spelling is a relatively unimportant subject and its aims are
rather narrow and limited. The latter characteristics, however,
serve to bring about a sharp definition of important educational
problems which other subjects present in a more general way.
One of these fundamental problems raises the question of just
what degree of perfection can we expect of school learning. When
the spelling gains of an experiment are evaluated according to the
norms of a well-standardized spelling scale, the result has the
advantage of objectivity, but it has also the disadvantage of
judging progress on the basis of what is, rather than according
to what might or should be, expected.

In the introductory chapter the results of Cornman's composition tests and the data obtained in studies of the correspondence
and compositions of elementary, secondary, and college students
were presented. It appeared that in compositions and correspondence written in and out of school, students spelled correctly
about 98 per cent of the total number of words written. The
percentage seems high at first glance, but upon reflection one
realizes that it means four misspelled words in a letter of 200
words. Viewed from that standpoint the performance is a sorry
one. Perhaps educators and laymen have taken spelling too
seriously, but as long as social and business standards of correspondence remain as they are, a short letter with four misspelled
words will mark its writer as illiterate. In common with the
fundamental operations of arithmetic, spelling must meet standards of strict accuracy.

The fact that life situations make strict demands upon spelling
has led some to assert that the schools should be satisfied with
nothing less than practically 100 per cent accuracy in spelling.
Because the schools have so seldom been able to achieve this level,
they have been subjected to much criticism by business men and

other laymen. This criticism very easily spreads to all education.

If the standard of approximately 100 per cent mastery is taken as the point of departure, the achievements of Woody's pupils in spelling do not seem so good. For want of a better phrase, a measure to evaluate results on this basis might be termed a "learning ratio." The "learning ratio" can then be defined as the ratio of actual gain in percentage of correct spellings to the possible gain in percentage of correct spellings. These ratios have been figured for the summary of Woody's data in Table 17 and are to be found in the last column of that table. In the fourth grade for example the initial difficulty is 54 per cent. There is a possible improvement of 46 per cent. The actual improvement was 22 per cent. The improvement ratio is .48. The average improvement ratio for the three grades is .52. To state the matter in slightly different form, this means that on the average a word gains one-half the distance to 100 per cent as a result of specific teaching. Or it might be said that, if the initial assumption is sound, the learning is only about 50 per cent efficient.

Evaluation of the Results of the Present Investigation and a Comparison with the Results of Woody's Study

The average learning ratio for Woody's results is .52 (Table 17); for the data of this investigation, .45. The difference between the two is probably more than accounted for by the fact that Woody's pupils had an opportunity to overlearn the words, and also for other reasons which have been mentioned. The very poor showing of Grade 4B, for which no explanation can be found, tends to lower the average unduly.

The figures of Table 18, page 46, lend themselves to a comparison of the results of this investigation with those of Woody's.

When the gains are measured according to gains in months on the Ayres Scale, the improvement of the Michigan pupils appears to be substantially greater than that of the pupils participating in this investigation. Our pupils gained only 12 months, while Woody's gained 21 months on the average. Of course, it must be remembered that even 12 months is a good gain for it was accomplished during a period of six months, part of which consisted of summer vacation.

The discrepancy between the figures of the two investigations is not real when a closer analysis is made. In Table 19 the words are grouped into three groups on the basis of initial difficulty and the averages and measures calculated according to these groups.

According to Table 17 the average of correct spellings for the words taught in the fourth, fifth, and sixth grades was 54 per cent, and the gain in percentages of correct spellings was equivalent to a gain of 21 months on the Ayres Scale. Now if the reader will

TABLE 18

Evaluation of Spelling Improvement

GRADE	AVERAGE PERCENTAGE CORRECT SPELLINGS		AVERAGE PERCENTAGE OF GAIN IN CORRECT SPELLINGS	LEARNING RATIO	EQUIVALENT GAIN IN MONTHS ACCORDING TO AYRES SCALE
	Initial Test	Retention Test			
2A	66	80	14	.41	9
2B	69	83	14	.45	10
3A	62	83	21	.55	14
3B	68	84	16	.50	10
4A	77	92	15	.65	24
4B	81	86	5	.26	7
5A	77	90	13	.57	15
5B	77	87	10	.43	12
6A	77	86	9	.41	11
6B	75	88	13	.52	16
7A	75	83	8	.32	10
7B	75	84	9	.36	11
8A	70	81	11	.37	..
Mean	74	85	12	.45	12

turn to the figures for this investigation in Table 19, he will note that, for words spelled with an average correctness of 57 per cent, the equivalent gain on the Ayres Scale was 19 months; in the fifth grade for words spelled with an average accuracy of 59 per cent the equivalent gain on the Ayres Scale was 22 months; in the sixth grade for words of like difficulty the Ayres gain was 19 months. The average gain in months on the Ayres Scale for words

TABLE 19

EVALUATION OF SPELLING IMPROVEMENT FOR WORDS GROUPED ACCORDING
TO INITIAL DIFFICULTY

PERCENTAGE CORRECT SPELLINGS INITIAL TEST	NUMBER OF WORDS	AVERAGE PERCENTAGE OF CORRECT SPELLINGS		AVERAGE GAIN IN PERCENTAGE OF CORRECT SPELLINGS	LEARNING RATIO	EQUIVALENT GAIN IN MONTHS ACCORDING TO AYRES SCALE
		Initial Test	Retention Test			
			Grade 2			
50–65	71	60	77	17	.42	10
65–80	99	72	85	13	.46	11
80–95	33	82	88	6	.33	10
			Grade 3			
50–65	124	57	78	21	.49	12
65–80	182	71	87	16	.55	12
80–95	49	85	94	9	.60	12
			Grade 4			
50–65	24	60	80	20	.50	19
65–80	82	73	85	12	.44	14
80–95	145	87	92	5	.38	10
			Grade 5			
50–65	29	59	83	24	.59	22
65–80	129	73	88	15	.56	18
80–95	142	86	94	8	.57	15
			Grade 6			
50–65	70	59	80	21	.51	19
65–80	142	73	86	13	.48	15
80–95	174	87	92	5	.38	12

TABLE 19 (*Continued*)

PERCENTAGE CORRECT SPELLING INITIAL TEST	NUMBER OF WORDS	AVERAGE PERCENTAGE OF CORRECT SPELLINGS		AVERAGE GAIN IN PERCENTAGE OF CORRECT SPELLINGS	LEARN- ING RATIO	EQUIVALENT GAIN IN MONTHS ACCORDING TO AYRES SCALE
		Initial Test	Retention Test			
			Grade 7			
50–65	58	58	71	13	.31	10
65–80	145	72	82	10	.36	11
80–95	130	87	92	5	.38	10
			Grade 8			
50–65	30	58	77	19	.45	—
65–80	58	73	82	9	.33	—
80–95	45	84	90	6	.38	—
			Summary			
50–65	406	58	78	20	.47	—
65–80	837	72	85	13	.46	—
80–95	720	86	92	6	.43	—

varying in difficulty from 50 to 65 per cent in this investigation was 20 months—not appreciably different from the increments shown in Woody's experiment.

For the second and third grades the equivalent gains on the Ayres Scale for the words in each of three classes of difficulty is about 10 to 12 months. The learning ratios, on the other hand, are somewhat lower than .50 in the second grade and somewhat higher in the third. The reason for the small equivalent gain in months will appear if the reader will consult the Ayres Scale. The words of Column L are spelled with an accuracy of 50 per cent in the second grade. In the third grade the accuracy has risen to 73 per cent. The words of Column R are spelled correctly by 50 per cent in the fourth grade. In the fifth grade they are spelled by 66 per cent. Thus in the fourth grade words of 50 per cent difficulty gain only 16 per cent in a year while in the second grade words of 50 per cent difficulty gain 23 per cent. An examination of other columns showing varying word difficulty will confirm the fact that according to the Ayres Scale the growth in percentages correct is much more rapid from the second to the third grade and from the third to the fourth grade than it is from one intermediate grade to another. Hence it takes a much greater absolute gain in percentages correct in the lower grades for each month of gain than it does in the intermediate grades.

The learning ratios in the two upper grades fall to about .35 on the average. The relative lower efficiency of the upper grades is in accordance with general experience. (Table 20)

TABLE 20

SPELLING IMPROVEMENT IN PRIMARY, INTERMEDIATE, AND UPPER GRADES COMPARED

PERCENTAGE CORRECT SPELLINGS INITIAL TEST	AVERAGE PERCENTAGE OF CORRECT SPELLINGS		PERCENTAGE GAIN IN CORRECT SPELLINGS TEST 1 TO TEST 2	LEARNING RATIOS
	Initial Test	Retention Test		
	Grades 2 and 3			
50–65	58.0	77.6	19.6	.47
65–80	71.4	85.8	14.4	.50
80–95	83.6	91.5	7.9	.48
	Grades 4, 5 and 6			
50–65	58.9	80.6	21.7	.52
65–80	72.8	86.4	13.6	.50
80–95	86.6	92.6	6.0	.45
	Grades 7 and 8			
50–65	57.9	72.8	14.9	.35
65–80	72.5	82.1	9.6	.35
80–95	86.3	91.0	4.7	.35

Two conclusions may now be drawn with the support of some experimental evidence. These conclusions concern the value of specific teaching of words in a regular spelling period when the school is a good city public school; the words taught are comprised within the first 5,000 of the Thorndike List and the method is approximately that of the Horn-Ashbaugh test-study procedure.

1. On the average, specific spelling instruction brings about, with respect to the words taught, a permanent improvement which is equivalent to one-half year's gain in excess of that to be expected as a function of general maturity and incidental learning. In the intermediate grades this improvement may be somewhat more than this.

2. Judged according to a different criterion the improvement due to specific instruction is about 50 per cent on the average of the improvement necessary for mastery. If mastery is the aim, then spelling instruction is only about 50 per cent efficient.

These conclusions may appear to be contradictory; nevertheless they are not so in themselves. They may, however, serve as premises for quite opposite inferences concerning the general health of the spelling situation to-day.

DISTRIBUTION OF THE LEARNING RATIOS WITH REFERENCE TO
INITIAL DIFFICULTY

In Table 21 the words of this investigation are grouped into four divisions according to initial difficulty. The distribution of the learning ratios is set forth for primary, intermediate, and upper grades in each of the four groups. The significance of the learning ratio may be enhanced if the reader will consider a hypothetical class. Assume a third grade class of 40 members, 75 per cent of whom spell the word "desk" correctly on an initial test. Under the test-study plan only those who miss the word study it. Therefore 75 per cent, or 30, of the class would not study the word; 25 per cent, or 10, of the pupils would study it. Now a learning ratio of .20 (as defined in this investigation) would indicate that of these 10 pupils who could not spell the word initially, there would be 2, or 20 per cent, of the pupils able to spell it six months after they had studied it; a learning ratio of .80 would mean that 8, or 80 per cent of them would be able to spell it six months after study; a learning ratio of .50, that 5, or 50 per cent, could do so, and so on. In other words the learning

TABLE 21

DISTRIBUTION OF LEARNING RATIOS FOR PRIMARY, INTERMEDIATE, AND UPPER
GRADES

RATIO	NUMBER OF WORDS			
	Grades 2–3	Grades 4–5–6	Grades 7–8	Total
	Group I			
	Data for Words with Not More Than 50 Per Cent Correct Spellings on Initial Test			
.00– .10	0	1	4	5
.10– .20	1	0	1	2
.20– .30	7	0	3	10
.30– .40	10	1	4	15
.40– .50	12	6	5	23
.50– .60	23	6	6	35
.60– .70	13	5	2	20
.70– .80	4	2	2	8
.80– .90	1	4	2	7
.90–1.00	0	1	0	1
Number of Words ...	71	26	29	126
	$Q_1 = .40$ Md. $= .52$ $Q_3 = .60$	$Q_1 = .47$ Md. $= .54$ $Q_3 = .72$	$Q_1 = .28$ Md. $= .45$ $Q_3 = .58$	$Q_1 = .40$ Md. $= .52$ $Q_3 = .62$
	Group II			
	Data for Words Spelled Correctly on Initial Test by 50–65 Per Cent of the Pupils			
.00– .10	4	5	10	19
.10– .20	8	6	12	26
.20– .30	16	7	14	37
.30 –.40	39	5	16	60
.40– .50	31	23	11	65
.50– .60	38	25	8	71
.60– .70	32	20	3	55
.70– .80	15	17	8	40
.80– .90	9	12	4	25
.90–1.00	3	1	0	4
Number of Words ...	195	121	86	402
	$Q_1 = .35$ Md. $= .50$ $Q_3 = .63$	$Q_1 = .43$ Md. $= .56$ $Q_3 = .70$	$Q_1 = .20$ Md. $= .34$ $Q_3 = .52$	$Q_1 = .33$ Md. $= .49$ $Q_3 = .64$

TABLE 21 *(Continued)*

RATIO	NUMBER OF WORDS			
	Grades 2–3	Grades 4–5–6	Grades 7–8	Total

Group III

Data for Words Spelled Correctly on Initial Test by 65–80 Per Cent of the Pupils

RATIO	Grades 2–3	Grades 4–5–6	Grades 7–8	Total
.00– .10	18	19	33	70
.10– .20	10	19	23	52
.20– .30	24	27	26	77
.30– .40	30	35	36	101
.40– .50	36	40	29	105
.50– .60	37	53	23	113
.60– .70	56	59	20	135
.70– .80	38	43	9	90
.80– .90	19	19	3	41
.90–1.00	12	3	2	17
Number of Words ...	280	317	204	801
	$Q_1 = .36$	$Q_1 = .34$	$Q_1 = .18$	$Q_1 = .30$
	Md. $= .56$	Md. $= .54$	Md. $= .36$	Md. $= .50$
	$Q_3 = .70$	$Q_3 = .68$	$Q_3 = .52$	$Q_3 = .66$

Group IV

Data for Words Spelled Correctly on Initial Test by 80–95 Per Cent of the Pupils

RATIO	Grades 2–3	Grades 4–5–6	Grades 7–8	Total
.00– .10	11	89	35	135
.10– .20	1	16	9	26
.20– .30	5	33	24	62
.30– .40	9	29	19	57
.40– .50	6	46	15	67
.50– .60	16	68	26	110
.60– .70	9	79	24	112
.70– .80	7	63	18	88
.80– .90	11	30	15	56
.90–1.00	8	31	5	44
Number of Words ...	83	484	190	757
	$Q_1 = .34$	$Q_1 = .25$	$Q_1 = .21$	$Q_1 = .25$
	Md. $= .56$	Md. $= .54$	Md. $= .45$	Md. $= .53$
	$Q_3 = .77$	$Q_3 = .71$	$Q_3 = .66$	$Q_3 = .70$

ratio may be thought of as the percentage of pupils learning to spell the word as a result, presumably, of class instruction.

A first inspection of the table discloses a disconcerting variability in these learning ratios, or in the gains that various words make as a result of instruction. The words of Group I—less than 50 per cent correct spellings initially—show the smallest dispersion although even here the quartile range for the primary grades is .20. The words are probably not numerous enough in this group to warrant conclusions.

For the words of Group II, in the upper grades the learning ratio in the case of 25 per cent of the words is as low as .20; in the intermediate grades 25 per cent of the words show a learning ratio of .70. In the light of expectation the results are chaotic. Under the test-study plan the pupils study only the words they miss. A reasonable anticipation would be that variability of performance would be reduced. The concentration of attack should lead to a weeding out of differences, unless there is a highly differential rate of response upon the part of the various words to the amount of learning energy expended. This hypothesis will be examined later.

It is significant that the initial difficulty of the words on the average has no effect on the learning ratios. That is to say, difficult words make as high relative gains as easy words. Absolutely the difficult words greatly outstrip the easy words in gains. On the average a word makes a gain one-half way to 100 per cent correctness no matter what its initial percentage. Woody also found that the hard words are retained remarkably well. This suggests the advisability of including more hard words in the curriculum. In a class of 40, of the 20 children who cannot spell a word of 50 per cent initial difficulty, 10 will be able to spell it six months after teaching. In the same class, of the eight children who cannot spell a word of 80 per cent difficulty, four will be able to spell it six months after teaching. In the case of the hard word, six more children have learned to spell it than the number who learned to spell the easy word. It must be borne in mind that the loading of the curriculum with harder words might result in lower learning ratios. As long as the educational world is content with considerably less than 100 per cent spelling of the words taught, the inclusion of more hard words offers the possible hope that more children would benefit by the spelling instruction. Some of the easier words might be left to incidental learning. The higher percentages of correct spellings for many words before study raises the expectation that these words might be abandoned to incidental learning entirely except in the case of pupils with special or general disability.

COMPARISON OF THE GAINS MADE BY SLOW AND FAST CLASSES

Tables 22 and 23 present figures which permit comparisons of the fast and slow classes from several viewpoints. In examining the tables the reader should bear in mind that the same lists of words were taught to the fast classes as were taught to the slow. According to Table 22 the average initial percentage of correct spellings for the slow groups of all grades was 61 per cent; the absolute gain was 16 per cent. The average initial percentage of correct spellings for the fast groups was 83 per cent; the absolute gain 8 per cent. The average learning ratio for the fast classes was .48; for the slow classes .40. Thus the absolute gain of the fast classes was only one-half that of the slow classes and the learning ratios of the two types of classes were only slightly different. As is shown in Table 23, the learning ratios of the fast classes are much higher than those of the slow classes when the words are grouped according to the level of initial difficulty. The apparent discrepancy between the two tables is due to the fact that the average of Table 22 includes the 439 words which were spelled by 95 per cent or more of the fast classes correctly on the initial tests. These words were not included in Table 23. The inclusion of these words in Table 22 accounts for the lower average learning ratios. The possibility of gain in the case of these words was slight and the chance of loss relatively high. All the words were included in Table 22 in order to show the effect upon the averages of too many easy words.

The figures of the tables referred to in this section must be interrupted with much caution. The reliabilities are low because the number of spellings is only about 30 for each word. Furthermore, when single classes are compared, the results must be considerably influenced by the kind of teaching the various classes had.

With these cautions in mind, it is interesting to note several significant features. If the reader will turn to the end of Table 23 where the results for all grades are summarized, he will note first the small number of words of difficulty below 65 per cent among

TABLE 22

SPELLING GAINS OF FAST AND SLOW CLASSES COMPARED

GRADE	AVERAGE PERCENTAGE OF CORRECT SPELLINGS		AVERAGE PERCENTAGE GAIN CORRECT SPELLINGS INITIAL TO RETENTION TEST	LEARNING RATIO
	Initial Test	Retention Test		
	Fast groups			
2A	81	95	14	.74
2B	90	96	6	.60
3A	86	94	8	.57
3B	85	86	1	.07
4A	79	94	15	.71
4B	86	90	4	.29
5A	84	92	8	.50
5B	85	87	2	.13
6A	77	89	12	.52
6B	77	96	19	.83
7A	79	89	10	.48
7B	86	92	6	.43
8A	84	89	5	.31
Average	83	91	8	.48
	Slow groups			
2A	71	59	− 12	− .41
2B	33	69	36	.54
3A	42	67	25	.43
3B	51	71	20	.41
4A	68	89	21	.66
4B	71	83	12	.41
5A	56	88	32	.73
5B	62	78	16	.42
6A	67	80	13	.39
6B	67	84	17	.52
7A	81	75	− 6	− .32
7B	65	77	12	.34
8A	63	75	12	.32
Average	61	77	16	.40

Note: The figures of the above table are based on only about thirty pupils for each half-grade and therefore have a very low reliability. The number of words is the same as in the other tables for this investigation.

TABLE 23

COMPARISON OF FAST AND SLOW CLASSES WITH RESPECT TO AVERAGE PER-
CENTAGE GAINS FROM INITIAL TO RETENTION TEST, AND CORRE-
SPONDING LEARNING RATIOS. WORDS GROUPED ACCORDING
TO FOUR LEVELS OF INITIAL DIFFICULTY

RANGE OF INITIAL PERCENTAGE CORRECT	NUMBER OF WORDS	AVERAGE PERCENTAGE GAIN	LEARNING RATIO
	Grade 2		
Less than 50 per cent			
Fast	4	50	.85
Slow	111	37	.43
50–65 per cent			
Fast	13	32	.76
Slow	42	1	.02
65–80 per cent			
Fast	35	20	.77
Slow	32	12	.43
80–95 per cent			
Fast	104	9	.75
Slow	35	− 27	− .50

Note: Fast classes—67 words spelled correctly by 95 per cent or more.
Slow classes— 3 words spelled correctly by 95 per cent or more.

	Grade 3		
Less than 50 per cent			
Fast	12	42	.70
Slow	243	29	.44
50–65			
Fast	14	30	.71
Slow	93	18	.41
65–80			
Fast	55	11	.41
Slow	60	10	.33
80–95			
Fast	236	3	.25
Slow	11	3	.20

Note: Fast classes—90 words spelled correctly by 95 per cent or more.
Slow classes— 0 words spelled correctly by 95 per cent or more.

TABLE 23 (*Continued*)

RANGE OF INITIAL PERCENTAGE CORRECT	NUMBER OF WORDS	AVERAGE PERCENTAGE GAIN	LEARNING RATIO
	Grade 4		
Less than 50 per cent			
Fast	3	38	.63
Slow	37	34	.57
50–65			
Fast	19	32	.78
Slow	60	25	.61
65–80			
Fast	59	18	.69
Slow	73	10	.36
80–95			
Fast	142	5	.42
Slow	89	5	.36

Note: Fast classes—43 words spelled correctly by 95 per cent or more.
Slow classes— 7 words spelled correctly by 95 per cent or more.

	Grade 5		
Less than 50 per cent			
Fast	4	47	.72
Slow	99	41	.65
50–65			
Fast	21	23	.53
Slow	98	30	.68
65–80			
Fast	58	14	.52
Slow	82	18	.64
80–95			
Fast	164	4	.31
Slow	31	7	.50

Note: Fast classes—70 words spelled correctly by 95 per cent or more.
Slow classes— 7 words spelled correctly by 95 per cent or more.

TABLE 23 (*Continued*)

Range of Initial Percentage Correct	Number of Words	Average Percentage Gain	Learning Ratio
	Grade 6		
Less than 50 per cent			
Fast	22	57	.88
Slow	68	33	.55
50–65			
Fast	64	32	.78
Slow	100	20	.48
65–80			
Fast	115	19	.70
Slow	126	10	.36
80–95			
Fast	174	7	.54
Slow	95	4	.29

Note: Fast classes—37 words spelled correctly by 95 per cent or more.
Slow classes—13 words spelled correctly by 95 per cent or more.

	Grade 7		
Less than 50 per cent			
Fast	20	39	.62
Slow	22	31	.48
50–65			
Fast	26	33	.77
Slow	54	9	.21
65–80			
Fast	84	11	.41
Slow	109	− 2	− .07
80–95			
Fast	150	4	.31
Slow	135	− 6	− .46

Note: Fast classes—84 words spelled correctly by 95 per cent or more.
Slow classes—41 words spelled correctly by 95 per cent or more.

TABLE 23 *(Continued)*

RANGE OF INITIAL PERCENTAGE CORRECT	NUMBER OF WORDS	AVERAGE PERCENTAGE GAIN	LEARNING RATIO
	Grade 8A		
Less than 50 per cent			
Fast	4	29	.45
Slow	31	30	.48
50–65			
Fast	13	21	.48
Slow	38	16	.38
65–80			
Fast	22	16	.42
Slow	61	7	.18
80–95			
Fast	76	3	.27
Slow	16	− 10	− .62

Note: Fast classes—33 words spelled correctly by 95 per cent or more.
Slow classes— 2 words spelled correctly by 95 per cent or more.

	Summary—All Grades		
Less than 50 per cent			
Fast	69	45	.70
Slow	611	33	.51
50–65			
Fast	170	30	.71
Slow	485	19	.44
65–80			
Fast	428	13	.48
Slow	543	8	.29
80–95			
Fast	1046	5	.42
Slow	412	− 2	− .15

Note: Fast classes—424 words spelled correctly by 95 per cent or more.
Slow classes— 73 words spelled correctly by 95 per cent or more.

the fast classes and the relatively large number for the slow classes. It will be noticed that among the slow classes the total number of words is fairly evenly divided among the four levels of difficulty, while the words as measured by their performances in the fast classes are concentrated in the higher levels. For example, in the fast classes there were 1,046 words spelled successfully by from 80–95 per cent of the class on the initial tests, and 424 more correctly spelled by more than 95 per cent on the initial tests.

While it may be argued that many pupils of the fast classes were probably excused from studying words which they had spelled correctly on the initial tests, it must be remembered that the routine of the test-study plan requires them to take two tests— one at the beginning of the period of study and one at the end. Thus the large number of easy words among the fast classes indicates the great waste of having both fast and slow classes study the same spelling lists even though the work is individualized.

Another arresting fact shown by the figures is the low learning ratios obtained in the slow classes for the words which were relatively easy on the initial tests. For all the slow classes throughout the school, the learning ratio of the words correctly spelled initially by 65–80 per cent was .29, and for the words correctly spelled initially by 80–95 per cent, − .15. This situation suggests that in the slow classes there must be a substantial number of pupils who are making no progress in spelling whatever. The evidence, of course, is indirect as there are no individual records at hand. But when the slow classes show an average gain of 33 per cent in spelling 611 words which initially are spelled correctly by less than 50 per cent, and when the same classes show an average loss of 2 per cent in spelling 412 words which initially are spelled correctly by from 80 to 95 per cent, the suggestion is that some of the pupils of these slow classes must be showing excellent progress while others must be at a standstill. When the percentage of initial correct spellings is small, the gains of the progressing pupils in the slow classes overbalance the lack of progress of the others; when the percentage of correct spellings is high initially, the better pupils are undoubtedly the ones who make this percentage high, and the small gain is due to the failure of the pupils who are at a standstill.

If the learning ratios are thought of as percentages of efficiency of the teaching and studying of spelling in the spelling period, it will be noted that at all levels of difficulty the fast classes far surpass the slow classes. Because of the unreliability of the figures, the results are only suggestive. However, these classes are probably representative of the same sort of classes in other large schools. As will be noted in the summary of Table 23, the fast classes seem to be about 20 per cent more efficient except in regard to the easier words where the superiority is about 55 per cent.

ARE WORDS CHARACTERIZED BY A LEARNING DIFFICULTY WHICH IS DISTINCT FROM INITIAL DIFFICULTY?

It has often been noticed that words of the same initial difficulty in a grade show varying gains in percentages of correct spellings after study. Horn [26] has remarked, "The frequency with which a given word is misspelled in a given grade does not necessarily indicate under present conditions the difficulty of learning that word." The great variability in learning ratios found in this study might be due to certain inherent peculiarities of words of such a nature that some respond to teaching and studying more than others. If there were many such words, initial difficulty would not be a satisfactory basis for the grading of such words.

Another hypothesis would be that the great variability in learning ratios among words of the same initial difficulty is due, not to inherent peculiarities in the form of the word, but to the fact that average children of a certain grade may not be "ready" for certain words while they may be "ready" for others. This theory would attempt to explain the matter according to the principles of mental growth and would seek the root of the trouble in the individual rather than in the word.

It may be objected that the two hypotheses put forth suffer from a dualism that is unjustified. They separate the stimulus (word) and the response (individual), when as a matter of fact they are one. It would be absurd to say that a word had inherent difficulty apart from the persons trying to learn the word. However, philosophical subtleties need not detain us.

The wide distribution of learning ratios of this investigation shows that as far as the pupils taking part were concerned, certain words responded to study and certain words did not respond so well.

Now the practical question of whether this varying learning achievement had its roots in the peculiarities of certain words, or on the other hand was due to other factors such as varying conditions of study or teaching, or that some words were written or read more than others during the period between initial and retention tests, or that the words were associated with certain intense experiences, or that the children of the grade were not mentally "ready" for certain words because of immaturity, may in part be answered by observing the performance of certain selected words under other conditions.

In each grade 20 words were selected—10 words having low learning ratios and therefore high learning difficulty; and 10 words having the highest improvement ratios and therefore low learning difficulty. Now if the 10 hard words show a small gain in percentages correct in such a scale as the Iowa Spelling Scale and the 10 easy words show a relatively larger gain, then there would be some reason to conclude that words varied in "learning difficulty" as well as in initial difficulty.

In Tables 24 to 29 such a comparison has been made. It was not possible to match the words of the easy and hard groups exactly on the basis of initial difficulty. It is believed that 10 words of each kind were found which were near enough in initial difficulty to give a fairly conclusive answer to our problem. If the reader will turn to the tables he will find that for each grade figures are presented for 10 words with low learning ratios and for the 10 with high learning ratios. In the first column the learning ratios are given, the word is written in the second column, the third column gives the percentages of correct spellings for the word as found in this investigation for the grade in which it was taught, and the other columns give the percentages of correct spellings for the words in the various grades according to the Iowa Spelling Scales. Each column has been averaged. Under the row of averages will be found a figure indicating a learning ratio expressive of the gain made in the Iowa Scale by the 10 words. To make this equivalent to the learning ratios of this investigation, the gain from grade to grade in the Iowa Scale has been halved and the ratio calculated on that basis. This brings it in line with the ratios of this investigation for they were calculated on the basis of the gain made in six months.

An inspection of the tables at once discloses the fact that words with low learning ratios in this investigation do not turn out to have low ratios according to the Iowa Spelling Scales. In the second grade, for example, the ratio of the hard words in this

TABLE 24

A GROUP OF WORDS WITH LOW LEARNING RATIOS AND A GROUP WITH HIGH
LEARNING RATIOS COMPARED WITH RESPECT TO DIFFICULTY AS
GIVEN IN THE IOWA SPELLING SCALES—GRADE 2

RATIO OF ACTUAL GAIN TO POSSIBLE GAIN	WORD	PERCENTAGE CORRECT EXPERIMENTAL SCHOOL	PERCENTAGE CORRECT IOWA SPELLING SCALES Grade						
			2	3	4	5	6	7	8
Hard Words									
−.17	best	71	59	81	92	96	100	100	100
−.11	three	73	72	85	97	100	99	99	100
−.10	can't	79	57	70	88	93	92	95	94
−.04	still	73	45	71	86	93	94	99	100
−.04	as	76	78	87	98	96	100	98	100
.03	sun	62	65	84	94	97	97	97	98
.03	top	63	68	83	97	99	99	100	99
.09	song	57	54	77	90	94	96	99	99
.11	corn	64	69	76	96	99	99	100	100
.11	cup	55	61	77'	92	95	95	99	100
Mean −.09	Mean Percentage	67	63	79	93	96	97	99	99
			.22*						
Easy Words									
.96	door	74	73	86	97	99	100	98	98
.95	sat	79	72	84	91	94	97	99	99
.92	am	76	68	81	94	98	99	99	100
.90	baby	61	71	81	95	100	97	99	100
.87	boy	61	87	88	98	99	100	100	99
.86	cow	71	76	83	93	97	98	98	100
.86	take	79	59	78	90	97	99	100	100
.81	ball	63	75	82	92	99	99	98	100
.73	you	62	90	95	99	97	99	99	100
.72	find	64	65	76	80	81	88	96	97
Mean .86	Mean Percentage	69	74	83	93	96	98	98	99
			.20						

* Ratio of one-half yearly increment to greatest possible increment.

TABLE 25

A GROUP OF WORDS WITH LOW LEARNING RATIOS AND A GROUP WITH HIGH
LEARNING RATIOS COMPARED WITH RESPECT TO DIFFICULTY AS
GIVEN IN THE IOWA SPELLING SCALES—GRADE 3

RATIO OF ACTUAL GAIN TO POSSIBLE GAIN	WORD	PERCENTAGE CORRECT EXPERIMENTAL SCHOOL	PERCENTAGE CORRECT IOWA SPELLING SCALES Grade						
			2	3	4	5	6	7	8
Hard Words									
—.16	meat	75	47	83	90	95	97	98	98
—.10	cleaned	71	14	44	72	82	93	92	99
—.10	lie	79	41	57	66	82	86	88	94
.03	here	71	57	75	88	90	97	98	99
.13	higher	61	24	48	69	84	92	97	94
.14	kept	58	24	34	68	76	87	92	96
.17	barn	58	46	70	85	99	98	97	99
.18	four	78	48	76	84	93	98	97	98
.18	throw	62	23	51	66	79	82	87	93
.21	brought	57	28	54	84	90	94	96	98
Mean .07	Mean Percentage	67	35	59	77	87	92	94	97
					.22				
Easy Words									
1.00	start	77	41	77	84	95	98	100	100
.97	bottle	67	16	49	74	89	96	98	100
.97	reached	63	16	45	74	79	96	97	98
.96	night	76	65	85	97	97	98	99	100
.95	wash	78	36	58	90	97	97	98	100
.95	forget	95	51	85	91	94	96	97	98
.91	fire	98	35	66	87	97	100	96	100
.87	cook	87	21	72	97	96	99	98	99
.83	each	58	62	81	98	99	100	98	100
.83	black	54	50	82	93	95	99	100	99
Mean .92	Mean Percentage	72	39	70	89	94	98	98	99
					.31				

TABLE 26

A GROUP OF WORDS WITH LOW LEARNING RATIOS AND A GROUP WITH HIGH
LEARNING RATIOS COMPARED WITH RESPECT TO DIFFICULTY AS
GIVEN IN THE IOWA SPELLING SCALES—GRADE 4

RATIO OF ACTUAL GAIN TO POSSIBLE GAIN	WORD	PERCENTAGE CORRECT EXPERIMENTAL SCHOOL	PERCENTAGE CORRECT IOWA SPELLING SCALES						
			Grade						
			2	3	4	5	6	7	8
		Hard Words							
−.19	soldier	68	12	33	44	75	87	88	96
−.04	rainy	75	15	25	51	71	78	88	97
.00	forth	77	36	51	76	84	88	91	92
.03	measure	71	3	15	60	74	76	93	98
.09	notion	66	11	18	49	75	83	94	95
.15	awful	54	10	11	50	54	70	82	83
.22	subject	64	11	19	61	81	94	99	100
.25	pleasure	64		45	55	77	86	97	99
.32	piano	53	11	25	61	73	86	90	95
.40	pupil	55	23	28	50	71	83	91	95
Mean .12	Mean Percentage	65	15	27	56	74	83	91	96
			.20						
		Easy Words							
.97	won	67	24	46	70	86	89	96	96
.96	tank	74	36	62	87	90	97	98	99
.89	jar	63	25	41	76	78	93	96	98
.89	wheel	63	26	57	87	91	92	97	100
.83	between	65	7	46	80	84	94	97	99
.82	quite	56	19	43	59	69	83	87	94
.81	wished	64	16	38	71	84	92	96	99
.81	lace	79	24	55	77	90	92	99	99
.81	agent	74	16	41	72	87	93	98	99
.76	raw	55	16	40	68	88	89	95	99
Mean .86	Mean Percentage	66	21	47	75	85	91	96	98
			.20						

TABLE 27

A GROUP OF WORDS WITH LOW LEARNING RATIOS AND A GROUP WITH HIGH
LEARNING RATIOS COMPARED WITH RESPECT TO DIFFICULTY AS
GIVEN IN THE IOWA SPELLING SCALES—GRADE 5

RATIO OF ACTUAL GAIN TO POSSIBLE GAIN	WORD	PERCENTAGE CORRECT EXPERIMENTAL SCHOOL	PERCENTAGE CORRECT IOWA SPELLING SCALES						
			Grade						
			2	3	4	5	6	7	8
Hard Words									
−.17	wrapped	70	31	43	66	68	84	85	85
.12	different	68	2	12	41	59	79	86	91
.18	circus	78	2	24	42	67	84	91	96
.20	local	75	4	17	40	74	88	97	98
.23	whose	69	9	24	46	61	74	86	93
.42	calves	60	1	8	36	61	69	79	87
.43	safety	63	12	18	28	51	60	60	73
Mean .20	Mean Percentage	60	9	21	43	63	77	83	89
						.19			
Easy Words									
.96	deserve	76	5	20	37	79	85	86	95
.93	shopping	74	7	34	49	60	79	83	94
.88	debt	76	3	7	43	60	71	89	98
.86	surprised	50	6	16	57	62	72	75	78
.86	sign	64	8	30	56	69	83	99	98
.85	intended	67	16	33	60	76	89	91	95
.84	final	69	15	18	44	61	86	91	95
.82	ribbon	62	14	36	53	75	88	89	95
.80	postal	59	9	23	52	79	91	95	95
.77	ankle	56	10	25	49	63	79	84	88
Mean .86	Mean Percentage	65	9	24	50	68	82	88	93
						.22			

TABLE 28

A GROUP OF WORDS WITH LOW LEARNING RATIOS AND A GROUP WITH HIGH
LEARNING RATIOS COMPARED WITH RESPECT TO DIFFICULTY AS
GIVEN IN THE IOWA SPELLING SCALES—GRADE 6

RATIO OF ACTUAL GAIN TO POSSIBLE GAIN	WORD	PERCENTAGE CORRECT EXPERIMENTAL SCHOOL	PERCENTAGE CORRECT IOWA SPELLING SCALES						
			Grade						
			2	3	4	5	6	7	8
Hard Words									
−.36	splendid	75	11	20	48	49	71	70	90
−.23	hasn't	70	15	24	46	63	75	78	80
−.19	pleasant	68	8	19	45	58	65	76	78
−.17	course	70	5	14	29	53	70	80	87
−.07	concert	70	2	11	26	55	65	77	93
−.01	excellent	56	3	4	17	28	58	60	74
.02	absence	60	3	8	23	51	71	83	95
.18	barely	62	8	14	26	38	50	71	65
.24	manual	55	14	15	38	50	57	80	90
.24	easily	59	3	12	36	50	73	82	86
Mean .04	Mean Percentage	65	7	14	33	49	66	76	84
						.15			
Easy Words									
.97	topic	68	13	16	48	69	86	92	98
.90	statement	60	8	27	50	74	84	90	94
.87	accept	54	4	6	22	55	75	82	95
.86	regard	79	23	44	63	72	77	89	92
.85	method	61	14	21	38	67	82	89	98
.84	system	63	2	4	29	49	69	84	96
.82	examination	71	6	9	18	32	67	72	85
.81	nephew	64	2	10	27	57	60	81	90
.79	error	72	3	6	12	37	55	84	89
.75	instruction	76	1	7	20	65	85	89	99
Mean .85	Mean Percentage	67	8	11	33	58	74	85	94
						.23			

TABLE 29

A GROUP OF WORDS WITH LOW LEARNING RATIOS AND A GROUP WITH HIGH
LEARNING RATIOS COMPARED WITH RESPECT TO DIFFICULTY AS
GIVEN IN THE IOWA SPELLING SCALES—GRADE 7

RATIO OF ACTUAL GAIN TO POSSIBLE GAIN	WORD	PERCENTAGE CORRECT EXPERIMENTAL SCHOOL	PERCENTAGE CORRECT IOWA SPELLING SCALES Grade						
			2	3	4	5	6	7	8
Hard Words									
− .56	argument	75	8	19	37	60	71	78	89
− .32	independent	72	17	32	44	62	74	79	89
− .21	theater	72	4	16	30	58	65	81	83
− .08	appearance	74	4	4	19	26	51	62	72
− .08	cedar	76	3	11	26	56	69	74	89
.04	acquire	51	0	5	11	29	31	59	81
.12	secretary	58	3	8	24	33	47	59	83
.14	foreign	50	0	0	14	31	56	64	84
.14	similar	64	2	6	12	30	54	69	76
.16	practicing	55	4	3	23	32	51	64	73
Mean − .07	Mean Percentage	65	4	10	24	42	57	69	82
								.23	
Easy Words									
.90	combination	79	5	15	31	43	69	74	90
.83	investigation	71	4	10	21	47	58	76	87
.78	organization	77	3	7	13	30	43	60	77
.76	knowledge	71	3	6	18	42	62	83	87
.76	democrat	67	10	17	33	17	59	71	86
.68	accomplish	75	3	6	31	47	75	82	92
.67	succeed	70	1	4	23	49	56	66	78
.66	equally	65	0	15	19	45	57	69	86
.64	excess	75	2	6	30	59	81	85	92
.58	excitement	69	0	7	19	33	50	59	76
Mean .73	Mean Percentage	72	3	8	24	41	61	73	85
								.25	

investigation was −.09 and for the easy words .86. The ratios worked out according to the Iowa Scale show ratios for the two groups of words to be practically equal, .22 and .20. This seems to be the case in all the grades. The only significant way in which the two groups of words differ is in initial percentages correct according to the Iowa Scales. In the second grade the percentage correct for the 10 hard words is 63 per cent according to the Iowa Scale and 74 per cent for the easy words, while the percentage correct for the hard words in this investigation was 67 per cent and 69 per cent for the easy words. A further examination of the tables reveals that while the percentages correct on the initial tests of this study show small variation as between the two groups, the easy words in each grade show a much higher percentage of correct spellings than the hard words do according to the Iowa Scales.

The conclusion must be, then, that low learning ratios are not due to inherent difficulties in certain words or to the fact that the children of the grade are not ready for their presentation. The concept of learning difficulty does not seem justified. Initial difficulty, subject to the limitations of response errors, seems to define the difficulty of words for spelling adequately for the great majority. This reservation must be made. There are a few words, which for reasons known and unknown, cause difficulty at certain grade levels. "Already," for example, in the Iowa Scale shows a gain of only 1 per cent from the fourth to fifth grade and a loss of 18 per cent from the sixth to the seventh grade. (See Ashbaugh [4] for others.)

CORRELATION OF THE PERCENTAGES OF CORRECT SPELLINGS ON THE RETENTION TEST AS OBTAINED IN THE FAST GROUPS WITH THOSE OBTAINED IN THE SLOW GROUPS

Evidence that there are not certain identifiable words which are marked by learning difficulties is found in the correlations of the percentages of correct spellings obtained in the fast groups with those obtained in the slow groups. In each grade the 100 most difficult words according to the retention test were selected. The percentages of correct spellings of these words in the fast groups were correlated with the percentages found in the slow groups. If the 100 words which proved hardest for the fast groups also were the hardest for the slow groups, a moderately high correlation should be expected. If the correlation was low, it would tend to show that the words which were hardest for one group were not the hardest for the other group.

These correlations are difficult to interpret. It must be remembered that only the 100 hardest words were used in each grade. This selection of words ordinarily would operate to lower the correlations. Due to lack of reliability of the measures, (the correlations are based on only about 30 pupils in each group), an unusually high correlation would not be expected. Certainly none of the correlations reported in the table is high enough to indicate that there is any close relationship between the difficulty of words in one group with the difficulty in the other groups.

TABLE 30

CORRELATION OF PERCENTAGES OF CORRECT SPELLING ON RETENTION TESTS AS OBTAINED IN FAST CLASSES WITH THOSE OF SLOW CLASSES

	GRADE 2	GRADE 3	GRADE 4	GRADE 5	GRADE 6	GRADE 7	GRADE 8
Correlations	.25	− .01	.50	.42	.36	.45	.42
P.E.	± .11	± .12	± .09	± .10	± .10	± .10	± .10

The wide variability of individual words even on initial tests is well-known. Ashbaugh [3] has shown that pupils in 20 per cent of the cases misspell a word on one test and spell it correctly on a second test. If the reader will turn back to Table 6 he will note that while the average percentage of correct spellings according to the Iowa Scales does not differ from the average percentage obtained in this investigation, the individual words show great differences as between the two sources.

CHAPTER IV

SOME CONCLUSIONS AND SUGGESTED CHANGES IN SPELLING PRACTICE

Large Number of Words Spelled by a High Percentage of Pupils Before Study

Of the 2,127 words in this investigation, 25 per cent were spelled correctly before study by about 84 per cent of the pupils of the grade to which the words were assigned. In the rapid sections, 25 per cent of the words were spelled correctly by 94 per cent of the pupils in these sections. Allowing for lapses which are in part unavoidable and for misspellings due to general and special defect, it is suggested that such high percentages indicate that many words may be abandoned to incidental learning except when the teaching of them serves a propædeutic function. Such a plan, of course, is a matter for further experiment.

Specific Instruction Brings About Substantial Gains

While the conditions of this investigation provide only the basis for a crude estimation of the value of specific teaching, some experimental evidence is presented to support the conclusion that a permanent improvement equivalent to one-half year's gain in excess of that to be expected as a function of general maturity and incidental learning is a conservative estimate of the value of specific teaching with respect to the words taught.

Degree of Mastery Attained Through Specific Teaching

If the aim of spelling instruction be mastery of the words taught, specific spelling instruction on the average is only about 50 per cent efficient in all grades except the upper grades, where the efficiency is only a little more than one-third. This conclusion applies with approximate accuracy to both the fast and slow classes when the initial difficulty of the words is similar to that of this study. The fast classes would show a relatively higher efficiency if the easier words were omitted.

IMPROVEMENT IN SPELLING RELATIVE TO INITIAL DIFFICULTY

Words of high initial difficulty make as great relative gains as words of low initial difficulty. The absolute gains of the hard words are much greater than the absolute gains of words of low initial difficulty. This conclusion is substantiated by the results of this investigation and that of Woody's for words spelled correctly by as few as 30 per cent. Possibly it does not hold good for words which are spelled by less than 30 per cent of the pupils. It should be borne in mind that the conclusion is based upon a distribution of difficulty of words found in this investigation. The inclusion of a much larger number of hard words in the curriculum is suggested for experimental verification.

VARIABILITY IN IMPROVEMENT

The distribution of learning ratios indicates that words vary to such an extent in the amount of gain they make as a consequence of specific teaching that the quartile range of learning ratios for a group of words of initial difficulty of from 80 to 95 per cent was 45, the median learning ratio being .53. (Table 21.) Variations for other groups of words and other grades are hardly less astounding. Some words actually disclosed losses after specific instruction; others made gains up to 100 per cent correct. The results indicate that it is well-nigh impossible to predict the amount of gain a word will make as a result of teaching from the percentage of pupils who spell it correctly at first.

LEARNING DIFFICULTY NOT SUFFICIENTLY IDENTIFIABLE TO BE DISTINGUISHED FROM INITIAL DIFFICULTY

In this investigation it has not been found possible to identify groups of words which are characterized by special learning difficulty as distinguished from initial difficulty. The wide variability in gains attributable to direct teaching among words of approximately the same initial difficulty does not seem to be due to peculiar characteristics of word difficulty other than those which also make for word difficulty in incidental learning. It is not denied that there are some words which fail to show gains normal to words of like initial difficulty at various levels of pupil development. It is only asserted that it is impossible under ordinary conditions to make up a group of words which will be identified by abnormal ease of learning or abnormal difficulty of learning relative to initial difficulty.

No tested hypothesis can be offered which will explain the variability of improvement found among words of the same initial difficulty. It is suggested, however, that this variability in achievement is due to a multiplicity of causes—lack of interest, the prevalence of bad habits of study, and weak and confusing reactions to the words taught, traceable in part to the large number of words assigned.

An important research would be one directed to find out whether or not words of great importance in the child's writing and speaking vocabulary retain the effects of specific teaching better than words of like length and phonetic difficulty, but important only in adult usage. Another experiment might yield profitable returns by determining how many words can be taught in a school year when the aim is 95 to 100 per cent mastery.

SOME IMPLICATIONS FOR TEACHING AND CURRICULUM MAKING

While readers may vary in their opinions of the precise state of effectiveness of spelling instruction revealed in the foregoing survey, most will agree that spelling practice has not realized the promise of the vast amount of research which has been done in the field. The state of affairs can hardly be regarded as satisfactory even by the most confirmed optimist.

There seems to be some grounds for making mastery of the words taught the aim in spelling. The general philosophical principles have been well set forth by Morrison [40], but this is not the place to advocate them.

There can be no degrees of correct spelling. The psychologist in his investigations may find it profitable to investigate the degrees of learning to spell a word, but the teacher and pupil must judge and be judged according to whether or not the word is correctly spelled.

Now the school provides a spelling period to facilitate incidental learning because incidental learning fails by varying degrees to bring about mastery. Does it not logically follow that both teachers and pupils should expect to arrive at the destination of mastery rather than that they should expect to be helped a few degrees nearer the goal? If the school does not demand that the words specifically taught be learned to the point that they can be spelled correctly by all except the few suffering from disability, is there any reason why the pupil should be inspired with what has been called a spelling ideal? If the school habitually demands less than mastery in the case of words specifically taught, how can it expect that pupils will be actuated by ideals of correctness in the writing they compose in and out of school?

This is not the place to argue such matters. To the reader who subscribes to the aim of mastery in spelling, the following suggestions are addressed:

In view of present results, the reduction by one-half of the number of words taught is not a revolutionary proposal. In the first chapter it was pointed out that the 1,000 words first in frequency and range as given by such a list as Thorndike's, or the Commonwealth List, were of such common use by every individual that they should serve as a minimum list. With respect to the second, third, fourth, and fifth 1,000 words it was argued that they were not common to the vocabularies of different individuals to anywhere near the same extent that the first 500 or 1,000 were.

Now if the first 1,000 words in frequency constitute the great bulk of the words common to the vocabularies of most elementary school pupils when they reach maturity, then there is no controlling reason for demanding the teaching of all of the next three or four 1,000 most frequently used words. Therefore, if the number of words in the curriculum were reduced to 2,000, the first 1,000 to be included might well be the 1,000 most frequently used, while the second 1,000 might be those words among the next three or four 1,000 most likely to be misspelled, or most likely to be useful in building up good spelling habits. What those words are would have to be determined by further research. It might be found that more or less than 2,000 would be the better number of words.

The chief reasons for advocating this reduction in the number of words taught are: (1) The large number of words which are spelled accurately by many pupils without study; (2) the fact that words on the average make gains which are only 50 per cent of the possible gain; and (3) the tremendous variability in gains made by words. By teaching only two new words a day the Cleveland schools were able to achieve substantial mastery of the words taught.

If the number of words is reduced by one-half, it would be possible to re-teach words the next year when necessary. Certainly it seems to be a fairly reliable inference from the results of this investigation that many words should be given a review one year after teaching—the review to be as thorough as the first teaching. In many cases a third such review would be advisable.

If the school demanded mastery of the words it specifically sets out to teach, and if, in addition, correct spelling were demanded in all written work, a limited realization of the ideal of correct spelling would be attained. The doctrine that the learning of each word is a specific matter tends to lead to the teaching of too many words. While the evidence is indirect, the data of this study indicate that the pupil's effort is spread over too many words. This is fatal to the development of habits of accurate spelling in some pupils, because under such conditions the school acquiesces in incorrect spelling in the case of many pupils. The range of good spellers need not be limited for they may be trusted to go ahead on their own initiative to more and harder words.

Reference has been made to the failure of the popular test-study method to prove its unquestioned superiority over the study-test procedure. Even its most enthusiastic advocates find its greatest merit in the saving of time. This claimed saving of time has been placed as high as 75 per cent. The reason given is that pupils do not have to study words they can already spell.

In passing, the criticism may be made that this saving is largely illusory, except possibly in cases where the instruction has been completely individualized as in the Winnetka plan. (When the test-study procedure is used in connection with a conventional school organization, time and teachers must be provided for the necessary testing and the study of the words missed. As one spelling is hardly a reliable measure of the pupils' ability to spell the word, two tests are usually arranged—one at the beginning of the study and one at the end of the period, be it a week, ten days, or a month. This routine takes considerable time and the necessity of going through the routine and meeting its requirements makes impossible a free use of the time saved.

If the time saved is not profitably used, the advantage of saving it is not altogether clear. Moscrip [41] reports the activities of pupils excused from spelling in the University Elementary School, University of Iowa. These activities comprised: (1) correction of spelling in school papers in composition, English, etc., (2) checking the library cards, (3) filing, (4) cutting out pictures for the bulletin board, (5) mending tears in books, (6) preparation of school talks, (7) free reading, (8) separating hectograph sheets, and (9) numbering pages of pictorial books. Some of these activities are no doubt educational, but others are of such a nature that many an excused pupil might think that he was being penalized by having to do them. Certainly mending tears in books is hardly a suitable reward for good spelling ability.

As an explanation of the shortcomings of effectiveness found in this study, it occurred to the writer that the trouble might lie in part in ineffective habits of individual study by the pupils. Although the method of studying words was well worked out by the principal and although the teachers attempted to build up proper methods in the pupils, the lack of constant direction of the learning common to the test-study procedure aroused the suspicion that the pupils tended to lapse into poor habits of study.

During the course of this investigation some supplementary data relative to the efficiency of the two methods—test-study and study-test—were made available. These data are not conclusive, but they support the evidence presented in the first chapter that the superiority of the test-study method is by no means established. This problem is being subjected to extensive analysis by another investigator; therefore, only a summary of results will be given here. The data in Table 31 were obtained in the same school from which the main body of the data were procured.

As in the other investigations the test-study method seems to be only very slightly superior. This inconclusiveness suggests that perhaps both methods have features which are valuable. What

TABLE 31

THE TEST-STUDY METHOD AND THE STUDY-TEST METHOD COMPARED WITH RESPECT TO AVERAGE GAINS IN PERCENTAGE OF CORRECT SPELLINGS

METHOD	NUMBER OF PUPILS	AVERAGE PERCENTAGE OF CORRECT SPELLINGS		GAIN IN AVERAGE PERCENTAGE CORRECT SPELLINGS
		Initial Test February 9, 1929	Final Test April 29, 1929	
Test-Study	1010	62.23	90.23	28.0
Study-Test	1011	63.93	90.13	26.2

the study-test method loses by having all pupils study all the words may be compensated for by the benefits of class instruction.

This investigation has indicated that the teaching and studying of hard words is relatively as productive as the teaching and studying of easy words and much more productive intrinsically. This suggests that the study-test method might be relieved of one of its disadvantages by applying it to hard words only.

If words that could be spelled initially by only 30, 40, or 50 per cent of the pupils were used, then the study-test method would not be so wasteful of time and the pupils would gain the advantage of class instruction. This is another matter for experiment. The efficiency of the test-study and the study-test methods should be tried out in connection with much harder words than those usually taught.

On the other hand, the advantages of the test-study procedure could be utilized in this way. Instead of testing the pupils on all words, a short test of well-standardized words could be given at the beginning of the year or semester and pupils scoring high on this could be excused from all individual study of words during the semester. On certain days they might take part in the class work which took up the difficult words. Thus it might be possible to have a combination of class and individual instruction. Two or three days a week might be devoted to class teaching, the remainder of the days to individual study with pupils of sufficient spelling ability excused from this individual work. Or it might prove better to have class instruction every day for one semester and individual instruction during the second semester.

The suggestions made thus far in this chapter are perhaps influenced by widely current assumptions and practices. The doctrine of specific learning may be in need of reinterpretation. As it is at present applied, it seems to demand too much isolated and automatic learning in spelling. After all, children and adults must learn how to spell many new words without going through a process of specific practice. Of course generalizing cannot go on in a vacuum. But, on the other hand, words may be selected and taught not only with the aim of mastering the specific words but with the larger aim of laying bases for generalizing and for securing better methods of study. The investigation of Gates [19], and the unpublished doctor's dissertation of his student, Alice Watson, raise the hope that pupils may be taught the ability to learn the spelling of words as he encounters them in reading and in other activities.   Thorndike [50] has expressed this promise in the following words:

> Spelling offers another interesting illustration of the need for more penetrating analysis.   There is evidence to show that much of the learning and relearning or prevention of forgetting of spelling comes as a by-product of reading.   Some individuals, including many of the better spellers, obtain during ordinary reading impressions which leave after-effects adequate to aid in spelling.   A method of teaching spelling which, other things being equal, improved ability to perceive words during reading in a way beneficial to later spelling, would be highly advantageous.   Indeed its influence in this direction might far outweigh its influence in the day-by-day learning of the four or six hundred words assigned for study each year.

BIBLIOGRAPHY

1. ALLTUCKER, MARGARET. "Research Improving the Teaching of Spelling." *Elementary English Review*, IV, 174–175, 1927.
2. ARNOLD, SARAH L. "The Mastery of Spelling." *Journal of Education*, Vol. XCIX, 186–189, 1924.
3. ASHBAUGH, ERNEST J. "Variability of Children in Spelling." *School and Society*, IX, 93–98, 1919.
4. ASHBAUGH, ERNEST J. "The Iowa Spelling Scales." *Journal of Education Research Monographs*, No. 3, 1922. Pp. 144.
5. ASHBAUGH, ERNEST J. "Non-School English of High-School Students." *Journal of Educational Research*, XV, 307–313, 1927.
6. AYRES, LEONARD P. *A Measuring Scale for Ability in Spelling.* Division of Education, The Russell Sage Foundation, New York, 1915. Pp. 58.
7. BALLOU, FRANK W. "Measuring Boston's Spelling Ability by the Ayres' Spelling Scale." *School and Society*, V, 267–270, 1917.
8. BAUER, NICHOLAS. *The New Orleans Public School Spelling List.* F. F. Hansell and Brothers, New Orleans, 1916.
9. BRANDENBURG, G. C. "Some Possible Secondary Factors in Spelling Ability." *School and Society*, IX, 632–636, 1919.
10. BREED, FREDERICK S. and FRENCH, WILLIAM C. *The Breed-French Speller.* Lyons and Carnahan, Chicago, 1927. Pp. 257
11. BRIGGS, THOMAS H. and BAMBERGER, FLORENCE E. "The Validity of the Ayres Spelling Scale." *School and Society*, VI, 538–540, 1917.
12. BUSWELL, GUY T. "Summary of Arithmetic Investigations," (1928). *Elementary School Journal*, XXIX, 737–742, June, 1929.
13. BUCKINGHAM, B. R. *Spelling Ability; Its Measurement and Distribution.* Contributions to Education, No. 59, Bureau of Publications, Teachers College, Columbia University, 1913. Pp. 116.
14. BURNHAM, WILLIAM H. "The Hygiene and Psychology of Spelling." *Pedagogical Seminary*, XIII, 474–501, 1906.
15. COOK, W. A. and O'SHEA, M. V. *The Child and His Spelling.* The Bobbs-Merrill Company, Indianapolis, 1914. Pp. 254.
16. CORNMAN, OLIVER P. *Spelling in the Elementary School.* Ginn and Company, Boston, 1902. Pp. 98.
17. FINKENBINDER, E. O. "The Spelling of Homonyms." *Pedagogical Seminary*, XXX, 241–251, 1923.
18. FRENCH, WILL C. "A Study of Children's Letters." *Fourth Yearbook of the Department of Superintendence of the National Educational Association*, 144–145, 1926.
19. GATES, ARTHUR I. *The Psychology of Reading and Spelling with Special Reference to Disability.* Contributions to Education, No. 129, Bureau of Publications, Teachers College, Columbia University, 1922. Pp. vii–108.

20. GATES, ARTHUR I. "A Study of the Rôle of Visual Perception, Intelligence, and Certain Associative Processes in Reading and Spelling." *Journal of Educational Psychology*, XVII, 433–445, 1926.
21. GATES, ARTHUR I. "A Modern Systematic versus an Opportunistic Method of Teaching." *Teachers College Record*, XXVII, 679–700, 1926.
22. GATES, ARTHUR I. and CHASE, ESTHER H. "Methods and Theories of Learning to Spell Tested by Studies of Deaf Children." *Journal of Educational Psychology*, XVII, 289–300, 1926.
23. GRUPE, MARY A. "A Review of the Pedagogical Studies in the Teaching of Spelling." *Education*, XXXIV, 1–19, 1913.
24. HILDERBRANT, EDITH L. "Can High-School Students Spell?" *School Review*, XXXII, 779–782, 1924.
25. HOLLINGWORTH, LETA S. *The Psychology of Special Disability in Spelling.* Contributions to Education, No. 88, Bureau of Publications, Teachers College, Columbia University, 1918. Pp. vi–105.
26. HORN, ERNEST. "Principles of Method in Teaching Spelling Derived from Scientific Investigations." *Eighteenth Yearbook of the National Society for the Study of Education*, Part II, 52–77, 1919.
27. HORN, ERNEST and ASHBAUGH, ERNEST J. *Fundamentals of Spelling.* J. B. Lippincott Company, Philadelphia, 1928. Pp. 148.
28. HORN, ERNEST. *A Basic Writing Vocabulary.* University of Iowa Monographs in Education, First Series, No. 4, April 1, 1926. Pp. 225.
29. HORN, ERNEST. "Uses of the Ten Thousand Words Commonest in Writing." *Elementary English Review*, IV, 167–171, 1927.
30. IRMINIA, SISTER M., et al. "An Annotated Bibliography of Studies Relating to Spelling." *The Catholic University of America, Educational Research Bulletins*, III, The Catholic Educational Press, Washington D. C., January, 1928. Pp. 56.
31. JONES, W. FRANKLIN. *Concrete Investigation of the Materials of English Spelling.* University of South Dakota, Vermillion, S. D., 1913. Pp. 27.
32. JONES, W. FRANKLIN. *The Jones Complete Course in Spelling.* Hall & McCreary Co., Chicago, 1924. Pp. 227.
33. KEENER, E. E. "Comparison of the Group and Individual Methods of Teaching Spelling." *Journal of Educational Method*, VI, 31–35, 1926.
34. KILZER, L. R. "The Test-Study *versus* the Study-Test Method in Teaching Spelling." *School Review*, XXXIV, 521–525, 1926.
35. LENTZ, C. A. "An Experiment with the Horn-Ashbaugh Speller." *Chicago Schools Journal*, IX, 135–146, 1926.
36. LESTER, JOHN A. "Delimitation of the Spelling Problem." *English Journal*, VI, 402–411, 1917.
37. LESTER, JOHN A. "A Study of High School Spelling Material." *Journal of Educational Psychology*, XIII, 65–74, 152–159, 1922.
38. MASTERS, HARRY V. *A Study of Spelling Errors.* Studies in Education, University of Iowa, Iowa City, Iowa, 1927. Pp. 80.
39. MEARNS, HUGHES. "A Report on a Specific Spelling Situation." *Teachers College Record*, XXVI, 220–229, 1924.
40. MORRISON, HENRY C. *The Practice of Teaching in the Secondary School.* The University of Chicago Press, Chicago, 1926. Pp. 661.

41. MOSCRIP, RUTH. "Meeting Individual Differences in Spelling Ability." *Elementary English Review*, IV, 172–173, 1927.

42. ORLEANS, JACOB S. "The Ability to Spell." *School and Society*, XXIII, 407–408, 1926.

43. PEARSON, HENRY C. "The Scientific Study of the Teaching of Spelling." *Journal of Educational Psychology*, II, 241–252, 1911.

44. REED, HOMER B. *Psychology of the Elementary School Subjects.* Ginn and Company, Boston, 1927. Chapter XIV, Spelling, pp. 224–272.

45. RICE, J. M. "The Futility of the Spelling Grind." *Forum*, XXIII, 163–172, 409–419, 1897.

46. RICHARDS, ALBERTINE A. "Spelling and the Individual System." *School and Society*, X, 647–650, 1920.

47. SEARS, J. B. "Spelling Efficiency in the Oakland Schools." *School and Society*, II, 531–537, 569–574, 1915.

48. SUDWEEKS, JOSEPH. "Practical Helps in Teaching Spelling: Summary of Helpful Principles and Methods." *Journal of Educational Research*, XVI, 106–118, 1927.

49. THORNDIKE, E. L. *The Teacher's Word Book.* Bureau of Publications, Teachers College, Columbia University, 1921, rev., 1927. Pp. vi–134.

50. THORNDIKE, E. L. "The Need for Fundamental Analysis." *The Elementary School Journal*, XXX, 189–191, 1929.

51. THORNDIKE, E. L. and WOHLFARTH, JULIA H. *Growth in Spelling.* World Book Company, Yonkers-on-Hudson, 1929.

52. THORNDIKE, E. L. and WOHLFARTH, JULIA H. Pamphlet. *Growth in Spelling.* World Book Company, Yonkers-on-Hudson, 1929. Pp. 44.

53. TIDYMAN, W. F. "A Critical Study of Rice's Investigation of Spelling Efficiency." *Pedagogical Seminary*, XXII, 391–400, 1915.

54. TIDYMAN, W. F. *Survey of the Writing Vocabularies of Public School Children in Connecticut.* Teachers Leaflet No. 15. Bureau of Education, Washington, D. C., 1921. Pp. 18.

55. TIDYMAN, W. F. "Do Elementary School Pupils Know When They Make Mistakes In Spelling?" *School and Society*, XX, 1924, pp. 349–350.

56. TIDYMAN, W. F. and BROWN, H. A. "The Extent and Meaning of the Loss in 'Transfer' in Spelling." *Elementary School Journal*, XVIII, 210–215, 1917.

57. WALLIN, J. E. W. "Has the Drill Become Obsolescent? A Preliminary Discussion, Particularly with Reference to Spelling." *Journal of Educational Psychology*, I, 200–213, 1910.

58. WALLIN, J. E. W. *Spelling Efficiency in Relation to Age, Grade, and Sex and the Question of Transfer.* Baltimore, Warwick and York, 1911, p. 91

59. WARD, C. H. "Intensive Spelling." *English Journal*, III, 484 ff., 1914.

60. WASHBURNE, C. W. "A Spelling Curriculum Based on Research." *Elementary School Journal*, XXIII, 751–762, 1923.

61. WOODY, CLIFFORD. *The Permanent Effects of the Teaching of Spelling.* University of Michigan, Bureau of Educational Reference and Research, Bulletin No. 71, November 15, 1924. Pp. 25. (Reprinted from Bulletin of Indiana University, April, 1924.)